12-YEAR-OLD READY

EXPERT ADVICE FOR PARENTS TO NAVIGATE THE YEAR AHEAD

EDITED BY
WENDY THOMAS RUSSELL

A READY GUIDE

PARENT **READY**!

PARENT READY!

2023 Edition
Copyright © 2023 Parent Ready, Inc.

Parent Ready supports the right to free expression and the value of copyright. The purpose of copyright is to encourage the creation of works that enrich our culture.

All rights reserved. No part of this book may be reprinted or reproduced in any form or by any electronic, mechanical, or other means, now known or hereafter invented, including photocopying, recording, and information storage and retrieval, without the prior written permission of the publisher, except in the case of brief quotations embodied in critical articles and reviews.

Published by Parent Ready
8 East Windsor Avenue
Alexandria, Virginia 22301
https://parentready.com

Parent Ready and design are trademarks of Parent Ready, Inc.

The publisher is not responsible for websites (or their contents) that are not owned by the publisher.

ISBN: 979-8-9865331-9-3 (paperback)
ISBN: 979-8-9880158-5-7 (e-book)

Bulk purchases: quantity discounts are available. Please make inquiries via https://teenready.guide

Table of Contents

Contributors v

Foreword xiii
   Sheryl Ziegler, PsyD

Introduction. 1

Chapter 1: Hello, Puberty 5
   How to understand what is happening to your child
   Janice Key, MD

Chapter 2: The Mysteries of Your 12-Year-Old's Brain 15
   How neuroscience can help explain cognitive and
      emotional development
   Rebecca Mannis, PhD

Chapter 3: Navigating Nutrition 25
   How to keep your child well nourished
   Megan Green

Chapter 4: The Nuts and Bolts of Tween Sleep. 43
   How to help your child sleep better
   Tyish Hall Brown, PhD, MHS

Chapter 5: The Importance of Movement 53
   How to encourage physical activity in a media-saturated world
   Wesley O'Brien, PhD, and Zeinab Khodaverdi

Chapter 6: Creativity 63
   How to lay the groundwork for innovation
   Craig Balfany

Chapter 7: Identity.................................... 73
   How to support your adolescent's self-discovery
   Joanna Lee Williams, PhD, MSEd, and Andrew C. Pool, PhD, MSc

Chapter 8: Family Dynamics 85
   How to strengthen your relationship with your child
   Karissa DiMarzio, MS, and Justin Parent, PhD

Chapter 9: The Power of Friendship....................... 95
   How to help encourage positive peer relationships
   Jonathan B. Santo, PhD

Chapter 10: Communication............................ 103
   How to have good conversations with your tween
   Andrew C. Pool, PhD, MSc, and Eden Pontz

Chapter 11: Resilience 113
   How to help your tweens learn to help themselves
   Lacey Rosenbaum, PhD, MEd

Chapter 12: Risk-Taking 123
   How to encourage your tween to make safe choices
   Andrew C. Pool, PhD, MSc, and Eden Pontz

Chapter 13: Navigating the ADHD Maze 135
   How to support your child and yourself
   Jennifer Gentile, PsyD

Chapter 14: Managing Chronic Illness 145
   How you can support the transition to adolescence
   Sarah Jaser, PhD

Contributors

Editor

Wendy Thomas Russell is an award-winning journalist, author, and editor. Following her career as an investigative reporter for a daily newspaper, she spent several years as the parenting columnist for *PBS NewsHour*, while founding a boutique publishing company called Brown Paper Press. She is the author of *Relax, It's Just God: How and Why to Talk to Your Kids About Religion When You're Not Religious* and the co-author of *ParentShift: Ten Universal Truths That Will Change the Way You Raise Your Kids*. Russell lives in Long Beach, California, with her husband and teenage daughter.

Contributors

Craig Balfany is a registered and board-certified art therapist and licensed professional counselor. His art therapist career included many years as an educator, practitioner, and clinical supervisor. Balfany's Adlerian theoretical perspective guided his work in educational, mental health, and community settings. He is actively engaged in the creative process that values exploring metaphors, encouraging expression, and building social connectedness through ceramics, sculpture, photography, gardening, and mask-making.

Karissa DiMarzio, MS, is a doctoral candidate in the Clinical Science and Adolescent Psychology Program at Florida International University and a predoctoral fellow funded by the Eunice Kennedy Shriver National Institutes of Child Health and Human Development. Her research focuses on parent-child interactions and childhood experiences of adversity.

Jennifer Gentile, PsyD, is a passionate clinical and child psychologist, thought leader, and mental health care innovator who cares deeply about improving the lives of people with ADHD. She is co-founder and Chief Clinical Officer at THYNK, which has clinically validated digital products that improve attention, impulse control, and self-regulation. As a practicing psychologist since 2008 at Boston Children's Hospital and Harvard Medical School, Dr. Gentile maintains a deep understanding of the urgent needs for improving mental health care access and quality. Prior to her role with THYNK, she led the clinical efforts to found Amwell's 50-state tele-mental health program. In addition to professional experience, three of her four children are diagnosed with the superpower of ADHD.

Megan Green is a registered dietitian with additional training through the Institute for Functional Medicine. With more than a decade of experience as a dietitian, Green is passionate about helping clients discover the power of food to enhance well-being and prevent or manage chronic disease. Whether assisting clients with making changes to eat mindfully, improve gut or metabolic health, cope with autoimmune disease, or something else, she always brings a positive approach. Green loves to learn and has fun challenging herself to try new recipes—even when they don't turn out! Recently, she is enjoying learning how to golf and downhill ski.

Tyish Hall Brown, PhD, MHS, a licensed clinical psychologist, is director of Behavioral Sleep Medicine within the Division of Pulmonary & Sleep Medicine at Children's National Hospital. She is also the author of *Navigating Teen Mental Health: An Expert's Guide for Parents*. Through her clinical practice, Dr. Hall Brown strives to improve teen success by strengthening their mental health and optimizing performance. She takes a comprehensive approach to treatment that incorporates the influence of culture, environment, family structure, social norms, and resources on adolescent function. Her primary areas of interest include behavioral sleep medicine, sports psychology, anxiety, depression, and coping with stress.

Sarah S. Jaser, PhD, is a pediatric psychologist who has been working with children with diabetes and their families for more than 15 years. Jaser obtained her undergraduate degree at Yale and her PhD in clinical psychology from Vanderbilt University. She is a professor of pediatrics and the director of the Division of Pediatric Psychology at Vanderbilt University Medical Center. In her research, she has demonstrated the effects of adolescent coping, maternal adjustment, and parenting on adolescents' diabetes management and quality of life. She is currently developing and testing interventions to improve outcomes in youth with diabetes and their families. These include NIH-funded trials to test a program to help mothers cope effectively with the stress of parenting adolescents with Type 1 diabetes, a positive psychology intervention to reduce diabetes distress and improve adolescents' self-management, and sleep-promoting programs for children and adolescents with Type 1 diabetes.

Janice Key, MD, is a Distinguished University Professor of Pediatrics, subspecialized in adolescent medicine, on the faculty at the Medical University of South Carolina (MUSC), where she is also the director of the MUSC Boeing Center for Children's Wellness. Key has served on many local, state, and national committees and received numerous awards, including the MUSC Distinguished Service Award and the Foundation Population Health Award, the SC School Nurse Association School Health Service Award, and the SC American Academy of Pediatrics Career Achievement Award.

Her life's work has been training future pediatricians how to best help adolescents and their parents.

Zeinab Khodaverdi is a passionate researcher from Teachers College, Columbia University, specializing in the field of motor development and physical activity promotion in children. Her work focuses on constructing evidence-based methods that advocate for healthier movement habits in youth. Her insights have helped develop strategies encouraging physical literacy and an active lifestyle among children. With a deep-rooted commitment to improving children's well-being, Khodaverdi continuously applies her expertise to facilitate their long-term health and fitness.

Rebecca Mannis, PhD, is a learning specialist with PhD training in Neuropsychology and Masters specialization in Reading and Neuroscience and Education. Through Ivy Prep Learning Center (www.ivy-prep.com) and The Mannis Foundation (www.mannisfoundation.org), Mannis consults worldwide with students, parents, schools, and other stakeholders to provide integrated educational support, enrichment, college advisement, and executive functions remediation to maximize educational success. Rebecca has used remote platforms for thirty years across the age span. She served on the Harvard Graduate School of Education Alumni Council in its first cohort of appointees. Mannis frequently presents and is featured as a media expert about brain-based learning strategies.

Justin Parent received his PhD in clinical and developmental psychology at the University of Vermont and completed his clinical psychology internship at the Alpert Medical School of Brown University. He is a clinical psychologist at the Children's Partial Hospital Program at Bradley Hospital and associate professor (research) of psychiatry and human behavior at Brown University. He is the author of more than 70 articles. His research is currently supported by grants from NIMHD and NICHD and has been recognized through awards like the NIH/OBSSR's Early Stage Investigator Award and the APS Rising Star.

Wesley O'Brien, PhD, is a senior lecturer in physical education and coaching science at University College Cork (UCC), dedicated to promoting physical activity among youth, stressing the importance of community, parental, and teacher involvement. His research in youth physical activity promotion, fundamental movement skills, and body mass index has been instrumental in shaping school-based interventions and policies. His research interests span the design, development, and sustainability of school-based physical activity interventions, along with physical literacy development. O'Brien also investigates measurement tools for physical activity assessment and studies youth sedentary behavior and obesity prevalence. He has presented at major international conferences and published in prestigious journals; he also evaluates postgraduate research students and undergraduate degree programs.

Eden Pontz is an award-winning journalist, media professional, and mother. She is Executive Producer and Director of Digital Content at the Center for Parent and Teen Communication at Children's Hospital of Philadelphia. She was Executive Producer at CNN's New York/Northeast Bureau, overseeing domestic newsgathering for more than a decade. She has reported, blogged, and created videos, podcasts, and written content on a wide range of topics including health, science, technology, and entertainment.

Andrew C. Pool, PhD, MSc, is a research scientist at the Center for Parent and Teen Communication at Children's Hospital of Philadelphia. He has a doctorate in public health with a concentration in social and behavioral sciences from Temple University and a Master of Science in evolutionary psychology from the University of Liverpool. He has worked in psychological and public health research for 15 years. His research interests include parenting, adolescent development, and effective translation and dissemination of scientific findings.

Lacey Rosenbaum, PhD, MEd, is an international psychologist with expertise in youth mental health and resilience. Rosenbaum runs the Mental Health & Resilience Group, helping schools and organizations improve mental health outcomes. Rosenbaum has led several national youth health initiatives for the American Psychological Association, the Centers for Disease Control and Prevention, and Mental Health First Aid USA in partnership with Lady Gaga's Born This Way Foundation. Dr. Rosenbaum is an adjunct faculty member in the International Psychology Department at the Chicago School of Professional Psychology.

Jonathan Santo received his PhD in developmental psychology from Concordia University in 2009. Santo is a professor of psychology at the University of Nebraska at Omaha and director of the university's Adolescence Peer Relations & Identity Lab. His research program addresses the intersection between adolescent peer relations and identity development, and he teaches courses in adolescent development, research methods, and statistics. He also serves as director of the developmental psychology graduate program.

Joanna Lee Williams, PhD, is an associate professor in the Graduate School of Applied and Professional Psychology at Rutgers University and Senior Director of Research at Search Institute. Her research interests have centered on race, identity, and racial equity in adolescence. Williams is devoted to using research to promote positive youth development and equity. She is co-director of the National Scientific Council on Adolescence and a member of the National Academies of Science, Engineering, and Medicine's Board on Children, Youth, and Families. She is an affiliate of Youth-Nex: The UVA Center to Promote Effective Youth Development and the Center for Parent and Teen Communication at Children's Hospital of Philadelphia.

Dr. Sheryl Ziegler is a Clinical Psychologist specializing in the treatment of children in private practice in Denver, Colorado. She is the author of *Mommy Burnout*. She is a news contributor on topics related to parenting and mental health and did a Tedx talk on "Why Moms are Miserable." She is the host of Dr. Sheryl's PodCouch and the founder of the parent-child puberty course, Start with the Talk®. She is an international speaker on mental health in the workplace and at home. Dr. Ziegler is an NBC affiliate Parenting Expert for the franchise series *Mental Health & Me*.

Foreword

Sheryl Ziegler, PsyD

For the past twenty years, I have been working with, treating, and, more recently, raising twelve-year-olds. I have supported thousands of families through the tween years, the middle-school years when your sweet child transitions into an official preteen and parents consistently say, "I thought I had more time…"

I understand, it does go by fast and the tween years can often feel like teen years, leaving parents feeling confused as to where to get information and support. Blogs, social media posts, or advice from a grandparent or friend may not always leave you feeling clear on what to do. This happens for several reasons—including the role of technology, more structured activities and less freedom to just be, and earlier puberty—to name a few things that are vastly different from when we were twelve.

So, when the editor of Parent Ready asked me if I would write the foreword for *12-Year-Old Ready*, I said yes without even having read the manuscript! And now that I have read the completed book, I feel humbled and honored to be in the company of the contributors to each of these chapters. Parents are truly, expertly, and lovingly guided to address some of the most important issues that pertain to 12-year-olds by gifted and seasoned clinicians and researchers with practical, smart, and updated advice.

This book is a true treasure that I gained great insights from and I am very excited that it is out in the world for parents to learn from as well.

Introduction

Wendy Thomas Russell

I remember precisely where I was when my daughter, Maxine, took her first step, tried her first solid food, and spoke her first sentence. In fact, I remember a lot about her first year—in part because so much of it was caught on film or video. It seemed like every nuanced advancement in those early days was both anticipated and celebrated.

Then Maxine started to grow up. And with every passing year, the "firsts" became slightly more infrequent. The camera came out less often. My memories grew a bit fuzzy. I don't remember exactly when I began to steel myself for her middle school years. I just know that by the time she turned 12, society had taught me to view the coming years with a degree of dread. Instead of anticipating exciting changes, it was as though the only thing we parents could expect was the unexpected.

That was unfortunate. Because, as it turns out, adolescents experience just as many exciting and monumental milestones as newborns. It's just that those milestones aren't always as visible—or as celebrated.

Until now.

As far as I'm concerned, the book you're holding in your hands might well be called *What to Expect When You're Expecting a 12-Year-Old.*

Written by experts in their respective fields, each chapter covers an important and fascinating facet of your child's rapidly changing physical, mental, emotional, and social states. The result is a series of touchstones that you can consult as you move through the year. To be sure, this book is not meant to be all-inclusive; if it were, you'd be holding a much heavier volume in your hands. And because kids reach puberty at different times, it may not reflect your child's exact stage in life. That said, if you have a 12-year-old and don't already recognize the milestones in this book, you will soon enough.

So what *can* you expect of your 12-year-old? Well, in addition to all the typical body, face, and skin changes that accompany puberty, you can expect a marked change in your child's eating habits (hello, Takis), sleep patterns (goodbye, bedtime), and personal style (how do you do, green hair, foul language, and cleavage-baring tops). You can expect to hear a little less about your child's day as their* gaze shifts—perhaps for the first time—away from family and toward their peers. And yes, you can definitely expect more screen time.

But rest assured: This is not a scary book. On the contrary, *12-Year-Old Ready* offers a wealth of accurate, up-to-date, and encouraging information, along with each author's own perspective on the typical experience of a 12-year-old child. Because this age comes with a paradoxical need for both parental guidance and independence from parents, the authors also provide plenty of gentle advice about when to step in, when to back off, and how to avoid common roadblocks. Conversation starters at the end of each chapter are sure to help you reach conclusions and decisions that work for you and your unique child.

Having raised a 12-year-old myself, I can tell you: Twelve is fantastic! I mean, sure, adolescence is a bit of a roller-coaster ride. Your limits

---

* The pronoun they/them is used in its singular form throughout the book because it is the most practical and inclusive approach.

will be challenged; your buttons will be pushed. You will sometimes want to scream into a pillow for a few minutes (or hours.) But, at the same time, it's genuinely fun to see our children act "older"—if not quite more mature. And it's exciting to see their identities take shape. Maybe your 12-year-old will be smart (think Scout in *To Kill a Mockingbird*), creative (think Roald Dahl's *Matilda*), or adventurous (think *Percy Jackson*). Maybe they'll be nurturing and responsible (á la Wendy from *Peter Pan*) or silly and socially awkward (like Greg from *Diary of a Wimpy Kid.*)

Whatever the case, just remember that all those sudden (and perhaps startling) left turns in your child's behavior and appearance during the next year belie a laudable truth: Adolescents are breaking out of your family's familiar routines and rules so they can become strong, capable, and self-sufficient.

So grab your camera. This is definitely worth celebrating.

Chapter 1
HELLO, PUBERTY

How to understand what is happening to your child

Janice Key, MD
Director of the Medical University of South Carolina Boeing Center for Children's Wellness

It's strange to think that even at the moment of birth, humans are programmed for puberty. Parents may not know it, but as they are teaching their children to walk and talk and play nicely with their friends, the entire complex process of puberty is lying dormant just below the surface. In fact, puberty is not so much "started" as it is "suppressed"—until years later when, much like taking the lid off a boiling pot of water, the brain releases a great, disruptive surge of hormones into the bloodstream.

The preteen years can be jarring for parents. Many have been lulled by the relative steadiness of the elementary school years, only to watch the little faces, bodies, and even personalities of their kids transform practically overnight. This stage of childhood takes parenting to a whole different level, and the stakes are high. After all, much of adult health depends on the habits established in adolescence. For this reason, it's important to understand what is different about your child's mind, body, and world and to use that knowledge to lovingly guide them to become their best self—healthy and happy and achieving their unique potential.

What is Puberty?

Puberty is the time of life when a child's body physically transforms into an adult body that is capable of reproducing and built for S-E-X. (And, yes, that means it's time for "The Talk.") Change begins when a tiny part of the brain (the hypothalamus) triggers another miniscule part of the brain (the pituitary) to send hormonal signals to the sex organs (gonads)—ovaries in girls and testes in boys. The gonads then produce sex hormones that affect many different parts of the body, from sexual organs to skin, muscle, and bone.

Hormones are molecules produced in one part of the body, then transported through the body to stimulate distant organs into action. Some hormones are thought of as male (testosterone, for example) and others as female (estrogen, for example), but men and women have both, just in different amounts.

Testosterone is made by the testicles in boys, by the ovaries in girls, and by the adrenal glands in both. In boys, testosterone controls the growth of the penis; development of sperm; thickening of pubic, facial, and underarm hair; and deepening of the voice. It is also responsible for glandular secretions (i.e., in body odor and acne), increased bone strength and muscle mass (i.e., development of the biceps), and increased libido (i.e., middle school crushes).

In girls, estrogen is made by the ovaries in a monthly cyclic pattern, with a sharp peak right before ovulation, when an egg is released into a fallopian tube. Estrogen controls breast development, increased body fat and fat distribution (to the hips and buttocks), and the monthly cycle of ovulation and menstrual bleeding. It is not unusual for boys to have some breast development during early puberty, but it usually resolves in time.

Notably, while "body fat" often has a negative connotation, healthy girls and women must have adequate body fat (more than 17%) for ovulation and bone strength. This is why eating disorders, such as anorexia, can cause periods to stop. Low levels of estrogen are necessary for boys and men to maintain their health and strength.

Physically Speaking

We are not entirely sure what biological events determine when puberty starts, but we know it's related to body size and fat content, as well as to genetics, such as a child's ethnic group and family history. For example, boys may experience delayed puberty if their dads did. And girls tend to get their periods around the same time as their mothers did.

As a rule, puberty begins at around age 10 in girls and 11 in boys but can occur anywhere between the ages of 8 and 14 for girls and 9 and 18 for boys. Girls essentially complete puberty—that is, start menstruation—about two years after the onset of puberty. Boys usually start puberty a little later than girls and take a longer time to go through the entire process, often still growing later, even after high school. This means that, at age 12, the difference between boys and girls can be particularly stark, with girls nearly as tall and developed as adult women and boys still looking prepubescent. When their bodies are changing so rapidly, preteens compare themselves to their peers and what they see in the media, usually worrying that they are not "normal." It is important for parents to educate preadolescents about the process of puberty. Let them hear the facts from you, not misinformation from elsewhere. Reassure them that they are on a normal schedule for their own body, and consult your health care provider if you have concerns.

Development of certain physical features is the most obvious outward sign of puberty. In girls, that means breast development, initially just enlargement of the nipples and area around the nipples, followed by enlargement of the breasts under and beyond the margin of the nipples. In boys, it means enlargement of the testicles and scrotum, followed by enlargement of the penis. These changes in boys and girls are quickly followed by the growth of very fine pubic hair along the sides of the labia or base of the penis and, after that, the growth of underarm hair. In addition to growth of thicker, darker hair in the pubic area and under the arms, sweat glands within the hair follicles activate, causing body odor and acne.

Height is another major sign of puberty. In fact, the speed of height velocity during puberty is amazing. It sometimes seems children grow taller each morning! But this growth spurt doesn't only affect height; every part of the body is increasing in size. In fact, the first hints of puberty may be a child's change in shoe size and nose size, as feet and noses are among the first parts of the body to grow. After the feet, the legs grow at an incredible rate. And the facial structure is transformed into an adult-shaped face, with noticeably larger jaws in boys. In fact, even the brain increases in size—first the ancient part of the brain that is the center of emotion, sometimes called the "fight or flight" area, followed by the "thinking" part of the frontal cortex. This is why 12-year-olds often have highs and lows in emotions without abstract reasoning, thoughtful discussions, and planning before acting.

Of course, puberty comes with challenges. Here are some of the most common:

1. **Acne:** It's the ultimate irony that just when a child becomes hyper-focused on their appearance, their face breaks out. The hormones that are produced during puberty have profound effects on the skin, including increased oil secretions deep in hair follicles. Clogging of the follicle with dead skin cells, oil build up, and the growth of particular bacteria result in acne: whiteheads (closed clogged pores), blackheads (clogged pores that appear black because they are open to air and dirt), papules (small red bumps), pustules (papules with pus in them), nodules (larger lumps under the skin), and cysts (larger areas of pus under the skin). Almost all teens have some degree of acne on their faces and sometimes also on their upper backs and chests. You can help them by suggesting a hygiene routine that includes face-washing at least twice a day (more if they get sweaty or dirty), as well as anti-acne soaps and treatments if needed. Over-the-counter topical products can be used to treat acne, including benzoyl peroxide and topical retinoids (metabolites of vitamin A). If that's not adequate, there are prescription products that may be used. Consult a doctor or dermatologist if needed.

2. **Crowded teeth:** Oral health is affected by puberty just as the rest of the body is. The growth of the jaw and palate may cause problems as adult teeth grown in. Often the pubertal growth spurt is a time of misalignment or crowding of teeth that requires orthodontia. At the same time, the mouth begins to produce thicker gingiva (the soft tissue at the base of the teeth), increasing the need for fastidious dental hygiene. Kids ought to brush twice a day and floss between and at the base of each tooth. In addition, they should have dental exams with cleanings every six months.

3. **Vision changes:** The eyes undergo growth that does not always occur symmetrically, sometimes causing near sightedness. Often, this is the age when glasses are first needed, again

just when personal appearance is at a premium. Because vision can change so rapidly, an annual vision test is needed throughout adolescence. If the screening at school or your child's annual physical exam turns up a problem (worse than 20/30 in either or both eyes), they should have a formal refraction by an ophthalmologist or optometrist.

4. **Body odor:** Twelve is an ideal time to start using deodorants or antiperspirants. While parents can no longer supervise bathing, they can check to be sure it occurs. At age 12, both boys and girls need to bathe or shower with soap at least once a day, washing their pubic areas, under their arms, and their hair. Be careful, though: Frequent washing with harsh soaps may worsen dry skin or eczema. As for the difference between deodorants and antiperspirants, the former fights body odor by killing skin bacteria with acidic ingredients and by masking odors with a scent. Antiperspirants decrease sweat (and therefore the odor-producing bacteria), usually by physically plugging the sweat gland with aluminum.

5. **Bone and muscle problems:** Rapid growth can cause unequal growth of bones and muscles. Issues can include scoliosis (curvature of the spine), a tight Achilles tendon (toe walking), and a tender, enlarged area on the leg bone (tibial tuberosity). Your health care provider should check for scoliosis every year at your child's annual exam. Otherwise, in general, stretching before exercise can help. Severe bone or muscle pain demands a trip to the doctor.

6. **Periods:** Many girls do not have their periods at age 12, but those who started puberty at eight or nine years old (remember, that's normal) usually do. When girls first start their periods, their bodies have not perfected this incredibly complex cycle. Therefore, they may have some irregular bleeding during the

first year. Some girls may experience sporadic bleeding, and others may see prolonged, heavy bleeding that poses the risk of anemia. While girls may have some mild discomfort when they first start their periods, they should not have severe cramping. If they do, it's time to make a doctor's appointment. All parents can educate their daughters about menstrual hygiene, look at menstrual products together, and have them available at home—ideally before the first period. Parents can also help girls by keeping a menstrual calendar together (there are many phone apps for this), taking them to annual exams, and having them checked yearly for anemia.

Healthy Habits to Start during Puberty

The foundation of adult health is built during puberty, particularly when it comes to bone strength and cardiovascular health. It is also a time when habits are set. In addition to helping your child address the various challenges named earlier, you can do your kid a big favor by using this time of rapid change to help them establish healthy habits for lifelong health. Later chapters will discuss some of these habits in greater detail, but here are a few important ones to keep in mind.

Habit #1: Sleep

Preteens need their sleep, no question. The recommended minimum amount of sleep for 12-year-olds is at least 8 to 10 hours every night. New studies have shown that the growth hormone activated during puberty is only secreted during deep sleep. That's right, *deep* sleep. What's more, we have recently learned that the brain "cleanses" itself at night, essentially clearing away molecular debris that has built up with all that daytime thinking. So watch that nighttime screen time, parents. There simply isn't a replacement for a good night's sleep.

Habit #2: Nutrition

Additional calories and specific nutrients are necessary for the healthy development of bone, muscle, and brain tissue. These include calcium and vitamin D for bones, protein for building muscle, and healthy fats and B vitamins for brain growth. Nutrition can be a tough subject because 12-year-olds are starting to develop their own opinions and may choose to limit their diets or become vegetarian or vegan. All kinds of diets can be healthy, as long as kids are meeting their nutritional needs and achieving healthy growth. (A healthy vegetarian does not live solely on cheese pizza.) If necessary, your primary health care provider can help you find a dietician with experience working with teens. Many teens (and adults!) are deficient in vitamin D and require a daily supplement, often with an added calcium supplement. Starting this habit when kids are 12 years old may help prevent osteoporosis in adulthood. Also, girls who have started their periods often need an iron supplement to compensate for monthly blood loss. Your health care provider can test your daughter for anemia to determine if an iron supplement is needed.

Habit #3: Exercise

In generations past, when 12-year-olds rode their bikes far beyond their own neighborhoods, adequate exercise was not a concern. Unfortunately, many modern neighborhoods are surrounded by traffic patterns that are unsafe for children riding bikes. As a result, we drive everywhere. That's one among many reasons why exercise must now be deliberately built into our daily schedules. In general, 12-year-olds should get at least one hour a day of healthy physical exercise—anything that gets them moving and their heart pounding. This can include organized sports, which have the added benefit of positive relationship-building, or individual exercise, which has the benefit of lifelong continuation. Physical activity has many physical benefits, including release of dopamine in the brain (kids learn better following a brief burst of physical activity), cardiovascular health, muscle strength, and healthy weight.

Habit #4: Annual health screenings

The 12-year-old annual well check is a pivotal time because it's when your health care provider can begin a confidential relationship with your child, meaning the parent may be asked to step out of the room for a moment. This does not mean you are excluded; it just means that your child has the opportunity to ask sensitive questions and receive honest answers. This is essential, as you want your health care provider to find out if there is a problem and address it early and to offer advice about risk-taking behaviors, such as smoking, drinking, and sex. Hearing good advice from professionals will reinforce what you are teaching at home.

Closing Advice

Although it may seem overwhelming at times, guiding your child through puberty is much easier than it looks. Sure, we live in stressful times—but most kids do just fine. And although they look and act differently than they used to, they are still the same child you have been raising for the past 12 years. So remember: You got this!

Conversation Starters

- I notice many kids your age are getting taller, some faster than you and others slower. Do you ever wonder about how old I was when I started growing and how it worked for me?

- Kids your age need to start taking care of their bodies differently. Let's go to the store and look at the different soaps, deodorants/antiperspirants, and other products to find what you think will work best for you.

- [For girls] Girls like to be prepared before they have their first period. Can I share with you how things work and what to do when you have bleeding? (Single dads might like to have a female relative or friend ask this question.)

- [For boys] Have you started to see hair in your armpits? Boys who have that may also start to notice changes in their penis and testis, and hair in their pubic area. Would you like to talk about what to expect next? (Single moms might like to have a male relative or friend ask this question.)

Chapter 2
THE MYSTERIES OF YOUR 12-YEAR-OLD'S BRAIN

How neuroscience can help explain cognitive and emotional development

Rebecca Mannis, PhD
Learning Specialist—Neuroscience & Education,
Ivy Prep Learning Center, The Mannis Foundation

"It's just developmental." These three simple words can either soothe or confound parents in the wee hours of the night.

Your child forgets their homework for the umpteenth time, despite your reminders and Post-it notes. Is it time to let them face the consequences, even though we know their brain is a work in progress, or do we keep issuing warm reminders? Is it our duty to guide our kid through the intricate process of maintaining friendships amidst the ever-shifting dance of social media alliances? Do we let our kid sweat it out when they come home frustrated about the format for their science experiment, or should we be letting teachers know that our kid is not really understanding their textbooks and how to juggle this week's football game and the deadline for next week's science fair project?

It seems like parents today face a conundrum when it comes to nurturing their kid's unique personality and providing guidance, given that their hearts and minds are still very much under construction. That's why, more than ever, parents need not just information, but also a community with which to share their questions and concerns. We need a sense of ourselves as the ones who know our children best. And because kids don't come with an operating manual, we need to delve into what neuroscience has to say about how kids grow at this stage, along with some benchmarks and tips for nurturing their growth in this era of emerging independence. That frame of reference helps us use what we already know about our kids as we navigate this next stage of their development.

TLC Framework

Many 12-year-olds are starting middle school or have already spent a year there. It's a time when schools are eager to let kids think for themselves and start charting their own course. But they still need our guidance, because any time there's a growth spurt, children need frameworks and boundaries to help them confidently navigate the choices and paths they encounter. Developing new skills often comes with switchbacks and speed bumps.

Now that your child is being asked to do more things their own way, it's crucial that we use our understanding of how kids grow and learn at this stage, both in school and in their relationships. We need to provide them with appropriate opportunities to take charge, while guiding them in a way that reduces conflict, shows authentic support, reflects our values system, and sets clear boundaries. Neuroscience helps in understanding how children's brains, relationships, and sense of self evolve over time.

In my 30-plus years as a professional and as a mom, I've developed what I like to call "The New TLC" for caring for each child. You might be wondering what this means and how it is going to help you when you're lying awake at night, worrying about your kid's summer reading. Well, by age 12, your child has already given you more than a glimpse into the detective work of understanding what makes them tick with this "New TLC." The truth is, some kids need the classic "tender, loving care" that is warmth, reassurance, and space to do things their own way. But, as parents, we could probably write a book on how unique each child is. This is where the 21st-century neuroscience comes into play with my New TLC framework.

T—Temperament: Each child has a unique, inborn way of responding to the world around them. We can observe their temperament pretty much from infancy. Think back; you probably knew whether you had an active little athlete or a serene dreamer on your hands. It's been 70 years since New York developmentalists Drs. Stella Chess and Alexander Thomas followed babies into adulthood to shed light on temperament. You won't be surprised to find that temperament stays consistent across the years, whether it's a child's natural activity level, adaptability, or tolerance for lots of sensory stimulation.

L—Learning Profile: This aspect helps us understand how a child makes sense of the world through their thought processes. For example, some kids excel at spatial analysis or memory (such as in math), while others have a knack for language. Those natural capacities—and areas that are less automatic—impact how they understand the world and how we parent them in middle childhood.

C—Culture or Context: This takes into account external factors that contribute to a child's growth, such as family culture, school environment, or community involvement.

Empathy and Expectations

Advances in neuroscience knowledge are happening simultaneously with a significant shift in how children experience the world and interact with each other. Gone are the days of the shared landline; now, it's all about unlimited phone plans and instant access to a fast-paced world. Even before COVID-19, children were already changing their communication patterns. On one hand, they were constantly texting and checking each other's social media, while on the other hand, there was a decrease in in-person socializing and parties. With constant access to each other, they leaned toward staying in touch in real time without physically being present. The pandemic only intensified these patterns. During COVID, kids needed to adapt, manage loneliness, and cope with the unexpected, which was quite a departure from typical preteen behavior. They checked in with each other, compared viewpoints, and started to notice differences between their peers' perspectives and their parents' opinions.

The constant exposure to information and updates left them feeling the need to process it all, align it with their own values, and cope with the relentless sense of immediacy. This complexity made it challenging for parents to strike the right balance between exposing their children to the real world and protecting their innocence. This is where our "empathic envelope," a concept first advanced by psychologist Dr. Ron Taffel, comes into play: Parents set the framework for family culture and expectations, while giving kids the tools to navigate the information, develop relationships, and make sense of the world around them as growing individuals.

Look around, and you'll see the range in height and strength among 12-year-olds. That variability in physical development mirrors the range happening in our kids' internal lives. Some are already navigating the complexities of preteen life and are savvy in their ability to read nuances or set the pace for fashion, while others are comfortable being their younger selves. Alongside appreciating this normal variability, parents should also bring the lens of the New TLC as you and your tween delve into the highlights of their 12th year, all tailored to your child's temperament, learning profile, and the context of school, family, and community.

Cause and Effect: A Stepping Stone Toward Abstraction

Your kid is ready to start charting their course for several reasons. First, they've had plenty of practice with sequential learning and experiences, whether it's basic math, writing paragraphs, or predictable evening routines. Also, the parietal lobes, one part of our cortex that is involved with sequencing information and visualizing how one step leads to the other, is largely developed at this time. Just forward to these lobes are the frontal lobes, which are still growing. These frontal lobes help kids practice sequences, reflect on their actions, and envision how to apply these sequences in different contexts. These and other regions of the cortex comprise the most human part of the brain. They *mediate*, or coordinate, the very *higher order thinking* and perspective taking that make our species unique.

As a result, your 12-year-old is beginning to develop a sense of abstraction. They can distinguish between primary and secondary information and visualize timelines, especially for activities they've done before. They might even demonstrate automaticity, working at a faster pace in sequences and abstractions. However, when they encounter new social, cognitive, or academic demands, these developmentally appropriate demands are bound to tap into less-developed areas.

Here's when we want to think about that T in the TLC. Remember how each individual is wired to have a particular temperament? Some kids are more impulsive, while others are slower to warm up. Some preteens are able to more naturally reflect and keep an even keel in the face of something unexpected, while others might become irritable, particularly when they are tired. This means that our kids will have opportunities to both apply those sequencing skills that are most natural and will also stretch themselves in terms of adapting to new needs and abstract thinking. Depending on where they are with those skills, the novelty of the situation, and other factors like their temperament, fatigue level, and the context in which they are having these new experiences, the process of connecting the dots is going to have its own personality.

The Changing Brain and Cognitive and Emotional Development

As your child approaches the age of 12, there are several important considerations rooted in neuroscience related to their cognitive and emotional development that will help you understand and support them during this transformative stage.

Hormonal changes and varied rates of development: Hormonal changes happen at different rates for different children. Some children may experience more pronounced hormonal shifts, which can influence their emotional responses and behaviors. See Chapter 1 for more on puberty and hormonal changes.

Neuroscience of emotion: Emotions are a significant aspect of your child's development, and many basic emotions are mediated by subcortical regions of the brain, such as the amygdala. The amygdala is associated with strong emotions like anger and fear. As you consider the TLC, you will be able to consider whether your child is slow to warm up, easily set off by disappointment, or able to let things wash off them easily. As your kid approaches adolescence, we have an opportunity to model for them, to manage our feelings as we deal with unexpected situations, and to provide insights and support as they find their way.

Social-emotional learning (SEL): Many middle schools have recognized the importance of social-emotional learning and have implemented curricula to help children understand their feelings and navigate social interactions. Think back to Descartes, who said, "Know thyself." Because children at age 12 are starting to increase their capacity for abstraction, schools and parents are able to help them start to identify what it is that helps them manage a task at hand or their feelings, whether it's around academic situations, self-perception in a challenging personal experience, or in their social interactions.

Metacognitive awareness: As children reach adolescence, their capacity for abstraction allows them to juggle understanding themselves as individuals with their own needs, priorities, and capabilities, doing so against the backdrop of fitting in. Metacognitive awareness, or the ability to be aware of one's own thought processes, becomes a valuable tool, allowing children to be successful and find their path as individuals, while also finding ways to develop and enrich friendships with others. Just as awareness of phonics rules in primary school leads to fluent reading and comprehension, the same thing is happening in the neuroscience of emotional skills for 12-year-olds. As our kids learn to identify their feelings and manage contexts, those insights become more intrinsic and internalized for them to use in a broader range of social experiences.

Special challenges or considerations: Various factors might impact your child's development at age 12, including:

- **COVID-19.** The pandemic may have affected your child's learning pace and their ability to grasp essential skills for middle school.
- **Personal/family milestones.** Changes in the family, such as a grandparent's health, an older sibling leaving for college,

or changes in the health of a beloved family pet can impact your child's emotional development and expectations.

- **New schools.** Your child may transition to a new campus or building at this age, which can bring both opportunities and stressors related to standardized testing and educational experiences.
- **Changes in curriculum.** Your child may face increased expectations and a more departmentalized curriculum. They must think abstractly and self-advocate while navigating various teachers and their expectations.
- **SEL curricula.** Schools have begun implementing curricula focused on social-emotional learning to help your child manage their strong feelings with greater insight.
- **Individual in context.** Be yourself, be a team player: Middle school emphasizes the balance between individuality and fitting into a group. Your child will experience a strong pull to assert their individuality while also seeking acceptance from their peers.

Closing Advice

Entering the age of 12 is a significant and complex journey for both child and parent. It's a time of remarkable growth, energy, and occasional setbacks. Embrace the New TLC model—understanding your child's experiences, supporting them, and knowing when to advocate for them or provide guidance. Development during this stage is hardwired to be discontinuous, far from a continuous line; it includes ups and downs. Your role is to maintain a structured environment while allowing flexibility for your child to learn from challenges. If things seem overwhelming, it may be due to this inborn and societally reinforced stage. Read: You and your kid are not "doing it wrong"; rather you are all facing this new milestone and the challenges inherent to adapting to this developmental stage.

> ### Parent Checklist
>
> ☐ **Stay connected:** Maintain open lines of communication with your child.
>
> ☐ **Break things down:** Give your child space to explore and learn from their experiences.
>
> ☐ **Encourage good habits of mind:** Encourage the development of positive habits and thinking skills.
>
> ☐ **Set an example:** Model the behaviors and values you want your child to adopt.
>
> ☐ **Allow for downtime:** Balance structured activities with free time.
>
> ☐ **Learn about classroom approach:** Familiarize yourself with the educational approach used by your child's school.
>
> ☐ **Learn about school culture:** Understand your child's school culture and how teachers communicate.
>
> ☐ **Advocate:** Be an involved parent when necessary.
>
> ☐ **Find your team:** Collaborate with other parents and stakeholders in your child's life.

Chapter 3
NAVIGATING NUTRITION

How to keep your child well nourished

**Megan Green
Registered Dietitian**

I'm sure there are days when it feels like your 12-year-old is talking to you like they're already 18. Even so, their nutritional needs do revolve around the fact that they are actually on their way to adolescence—a time when the body's rate of growth increases so much that it's second only to the growth that happens in the first year of life.

You likely have an idea, through common knowledge and personal experience (and also the previous chapter), of the changes that happen as puberty begins. In case, for one reason or another, you have blocked out some of those memories, this is when your kid may begin showing physical signs of sexual development and facial hair and enhanced emotions related to hormone changes, which can occasionally feel like a wild roller-coaster ride.

Let's start with a few general health facts. At 12 years of age, children technically fall into the adolescent stage of life (11 to 21 years of age) and the subcategory of early adolescence (10 to 13 years of age). Puberty marks the onset of the growth spurt. It's more common for girls to begin their growth spurts earlier than boys, but it does vary from person to person. This is why the nutrient needs of each 12-year-old are based on their body size, physical activity level, and whether or not they have started puberty. If they play sports, they'll need more calories and nutrients when they are active than when they are not.

Every five years, the Dietary Guidelines for Americans are updated by the Departments of Agriculture and Health and Human Services. The latest version was updated in 2020. This is helpful guidance at all stages of life. Below are the recommendations for children and adolescents ages 9 through 13, followed by a few highlighted nutrients.

Total daily calories

Females: 1,400–2,200 calories

Males: 1,600–2,600 calories

Daily servings per food category:

Vegetables: 1.5–3.5 cups

Fruits: 1.5–2 cups

Grains: 5–9 ounces

Dairy: 3 cups (or dairy alternatives)

Protein: 4–6.5 ounces

Oils: 1–2.5 tablespoons

Water: 6–8 cups

Protein

Protein is important for every cell in the body and is digested slowly, which helps provide stable energy and maintain fullness longer. In my experience with clients over the years, the most common thing missing from a standard breakfast at all ages is adequate protein. Getting adequate protein at breakfast can help avoid the blood sugar roller coaster and help your 12-year-old maintain better energy and focus in school. Research shows that a higher protein intake early in the day leads to less sugar cravings later in the day and better sleep. Here are a few helpful tips for protein intake:

1. A 3-ounce serving of meat is around the size of the palm of your (adult) hand. This is a good reference to use for portion size. Remember, the total recommended amount of protein for a 12-year-old is 4–6.5 ounces per day.

2. Besides meat, other good sources of protein include seafood, eggs, nuts, seeds, lentils, and beans. Fun fact: Cruciferous veggies like broccoli, cauliflower, and Brussels sprouts contain about 2 grams of protein per cup.

3. A simple formula to use when meal planning for yourself and your family:

    carb + protein + fat = every meal & snack

4. Teach this formula to your kids and use it together when creating a meal plan or choosing what to eat on the spot. Aim to include all three parts of the formula at every meal and snack. Examples of food sources in each category:

    Carbohydrate: *fruit, potatoes, grains (oats, rice, pasta, tortilla, bread), beans, vegetables, yogurt*

Fat: *avocado, olives, nuts and nut butters, sunflower seeds, chia seeds, ground flaxseed, extra-virgin olive oil*

Protein: *see #2 on page 27*

5. High-protein breakfast ideas:

   - Breakfast sausage: Try precooking a homemade mixture of ground meat and spices so it's easy to reheat during the morning rush.
   - Eggs: Scrambled, omelet-style, hard-boiled, or prepped-ahead egg bites in a muffin pan all make a great combo with fresh fruit on the side.
   - Toast with a cooked egg + cheese + smashed avocado or guacamole
   - Greek yogurt mixed with fruit + a scoop of nut butter
   - Protein oatmeal: Add nuts, nut butter, or milk to regular oats. Some brands sell a high-protein version, too.
   - Smoothie: Blend it the night before and give it a quick stir in the morning. Choose from a variety of protein sources. Good options are nuts, seeds, nut butter, milk, and yogurt. (Hint: Greek yogurt contains even higher protein because of its straining process.) Keep the fruit to ~1/2 cup. Hint: Blending in avocado will make it creamier and add more brain-supporting healthy fat!
   - Cottage cheese with fruit + sunflower seeds or nuts
   - Homemade energy bites: A combo of oats, nut butter, honey, protein powder, cinnamon, and a seed or dried fruit. Mix ingredients in a bowl and roll into balls. Sometimes these taste even better if stored in the fridge.

- Whatever protein source your 12-year-old will eat. Chicken breast for breakfast? Canned tuna? Beans? Sounds good. "Breakfast foods" are just a marketing tactic. Any food can be a breakfast food.

6. If your 12-year-old is on the way to play a sport soon after eating, try to get them a good protein source **at least one hour prior to the start of physical activity.** Because protein takes longer to digest, physical activity too soon after ingestion can cause an upset stomach and make it harder to play their best.

Importance of Iron

Iron is important in all stages of life, but for 12-year-old males, it's necessary to support expansion of muscle and blood volume. For females, it's especially important if they've began their menstrual cycle (period). The technical term for a female's first menstrual cycle is "menarche." Menarche can happen between 9 and 16 years old, but the average age is 12.4 years. Iron intake is important because iron is depleted through blood loss during a period, which increases the risk of iron deficiency anemia.

Recommended daily amount of iron for 9- to 13-year-olds: 8 milligrams (mg)

Common Food Sources of Iron	
Food	Iron amount (mg)
Beef (3 oz.)	2.5
Turkey leg (3 oz.)	2.0
Shrimp (3 oz.)	1.8
Spinach, cooked (1 cup)	6.4
White beans, cooked (1/2 cup)	3.3
Black beans, cooked (1/2 cup)	1.8

Common Food Sources of Iron	
Food	Iron amount (mg)
Sweet potato, cooked (1 cup)	1.8
Prune juice, 100% (1 cup)	3.0
Cashews (1 oz.)	1.9
Chicken breast (1 cup)	1.5
Eggs (2 whole)	1.4
Almonds, walnuts, pecans (1/4 cup)	0.8–1.3

Bonus: Vitamin C enhances absorption of iron from food. I like to call iron + vitamin C the dynamic duo. So, pair iron food sources with vitamin C food sources when you can. Foods high in vitamin C include red and yellow bell peppers, strawberries, oranges, tomatoes, potatoes, broccoli, and cauliflower.

Food for Thought: The Influence of Environment

Not only is your 12-year-old's internal environment rapidly changing, but it's also likely their external environment is doing the same. Take a moment to think about what is changing in their external environment. This may include:

- Going to a new school, integrating with new kids from other schools
- Riding a new bus to school, where they're now the "little fish"
- Being around older kids who expose them to body image conversations
- Experiencing longer school days that involve independently navigating the halls between classes
- Ramping up extracurricular activity duration and frequency (sports, band, choir, clubs)

- Having new, expanded school lunch options
- Being home alone after school for the first time or for longer periods of time
- Having less consistency in their daily schedule
- Having less time at home and less access to food options if not prepped

Thinking about your child's experience helps with one of the most important aspects of our lifelong nutrition behaviors—**awareness.** Being aware of what you like to eat, how foods make you feel, and how your daily schedule impacts what you eat will set you and your 12-year-old up for nutrition success.

The amount of nutrition education your child will receive in school is hard to predict. Funding for nutrition classes varies widely, resulting in potentially little to no nutrition or cooking education. A general health class may introduce them to nutrition information using the USDA MyPlate Guidelines, which is a helpful visual to use at home with meals. It recommends filling half the plate with fruits and vegetables at every meal. Check out more info at MyPlate.gov.

Below are some common issues parents face with their adolescents' eating habits and some solutions to try.

"My 12-year-old..."	
Behavior	Possible Solution
Refuses to try new foods.	Lead by example. Share that you're trying a food for the first time with them. Be honest about how you feel about the taste. Consistently offer various new foods to increase the likelihood that your child will try them.
Mainly eats highly processed foods or fast food, so I'm concerned they're not getting enough nutrients.	Your child eats what's available, and because you can't control all of their options outside of the home, optimize their options in the home. Consider something like the 80/20 rule—stock the kitchen with 80% nutrient-dense foods and 20% of the processed foods they're asking for (customize those percentages in a way that makes sense for your family's healthy eating goals). This allows them to have choices and isn't restrictive, which promotes a healthy relationship with food.

"My 12-year-old…"	
Behavior	Possible Solution
Always asks, "What's for dinner?"	Don't let this question stress you out! When life is extra-busy, you're probably already planning ahead in many ways to coordinate schedules, carpooling, homework time, and more. Put creating a weekly meal plan in the top 3 on your priority list. The more homemade meals you serve, the more likely your child is to eat nutrient-dense foods. Meal planning will reward you with money saved, less stress, and better health.
Is always hungry.	For the next few years, your child's calorie needs are likely the highest they will ever be in terms of regular growth and health. A common adolescent behavior is to graze on snacks often when at home. Encourage them to eat three balanced meals every day. Exemplify this process. Eat together. Use the recommended servings per food category listed earlier in this chapter to see if they are getting the minimum amount per food group. Start by filling in what they are missing to see if they feel better nourished.

| "My 12-year-old..." ||
Behavior	Possible Solution
Is busy going from one activity to another most nights of the week.	This requires good planning, especially if there are multiple kids with activities. Make a simple meal plan on the weekend. Are you in the car basically all evening? Try the car-cooler method: Pack a cooler ahead of time with snacks and meals that support good energy. Instead of rushing through the fast-food drive-thru, see if you can enjoy dinner together in the car as a family. If there's time, pull into a park and open all the doors. Turn on some music. Converse. Make it fun.
Is skipping breakfast on school days.	Breakfast is important for preteens, so plan ahead with recipes that are easy to reheat in the morning or for your 12-year-old to throw together on their own. Use the carb + protein + fat method (page 27).

Kids in the Kitchen

One of the best things you can do to influence your kid's current food patterns and preferences, *and* benefit their health in the future, is to get them involved in the entire process of what they eat. Start by asking them about their food preferences. Which foods, meals, flavors, spices do they like? Which do they dislike? (Ask yourself this, too, if it's been awhile since you've thought about it.) Next, get them involved in choosing the meals and snacks to have around your home. This makes them more likely to actually eat the food available to them (which means less wasted food and less wasted money on uneaten food). Then, figure out how you can get them involved in preparation.

Ways to Get Your Child Involved:

- Bring them grocery shopping.
- Ask them to help you unload and put away the groceries to spark interest in what's available.
- Assign them the task of washing the fresh produce. Teach them how to cut fresh produce and store it in the fridge properly so it's snack-ready.
- Invite them to help with cooking, such as stirring the sauce on the stove, beating eggs in a bowl, tossing greens with olive oil, or alerting you when the water is boiling for pasta.
- Make them your taste-tester whenever you're preparing something. This is one thing I can bet they will do without complaint!
- Eat together as much as possible, even if that means just the two of you. A higher frequency of family meals eaten together is associated with higher intake of fruits, vegetables, whole grains, and nutrient-dense foods in adolescents.
- Let them choose a few foods to grow together if you have a garden.

If you've already started involving your child in the cooking process, some of these tasks may seem too simple, so take a few minutes to brainstorm some strategies for involvement that will work best for your family.

Positive Vibes Related to Food

As you're probably aware, kids are impressionable at any age and especially at this age. Along with that, their independent time and thoughts, preferences, and opinions are on the rise. Although your kids may have heard your personal opinion on topics like nutrition, health, and body image before this age, *now* is the time when they will begin to be introduced to a variety of outside messages related to this topic. The prevalence of disordered eating patterns increases in adolescence. Researchers have found positive associations between young adolescents who are satisfied with their bodies and parents who are nurturing and supportive. Your own attitude and the words you use around nutrition, food, and health will be more important than ever.

My intention isn't to put pressure on you, but instead to inspire self-reflection that will help you in the long run. Imagine if your child is constantly hearing negative messages about eating or about a need to restrict foods from the people they look up to the most. We each have our own unique food story that's comprised of our important family and cultural food traditions, preferences, knowledge, and beliefs. What is yours? If you've never thought about this before, you might answer these questions in your head or on paper:

- What was your relationship with food growing up?
- Did you always have food around or were you worried about eating what was available before your siblings or other family members did?
- Did you eat food together as a family regularly? If so, was it a positive experience or were family members complaining about their days or arguing as you all rushed to leave the table as soon as possible?
- At what age, if at all, did you get included in the cooking process?

- Does your family have any traditions related to food that are important to you?
- Do you follow any cultural food practices?

Talking Tips to Promote a Positive Relationship to Food	
Avoid statements such as:	Use statements such as:
"[insert food] will make you fat!"	**"Wow! That meal was PACKED with flavor!"**
"[insert food] will make me fat!"	**"[insert food] has vitamin C, which helps your body fight sicknesses."**
"[insert food] is bad."	
"You shouldn't eat that!"	"We are eating this for dinner because we want to make sure we stay healthy!"
"I feel huge after eating that."	
"Just eat it."	"Let's try a new recipe! It's okay if it doesn't turn out perfect."
"You are being so picky!"	"That was a nourishing meal."

If you're concerned that your child is showing signs of an eating disorder, reach out to their pediatrician right away. Potential signs include changes in eating behaviors, taking longer than usual to eat, not eating what the rest of the family eats, avoiding events with food, making negative comments about their own body, displaying an excessive focus on food, regularly going to the bathroom after eating, and major physical changes such as hair loss. (This is not a comprehensive list; if interested, seek guidance from an eating disorder specialist.)

Why Sugar-Sweetened Beverages Aren't So Sweet for Health

Sugar-sweetened beverages (SSBs, for short) are the number one source of added sugar for *all* age groups in the American diet, and especially in youth. Why do we care? High added sugar intake is associated with an increased risk of obesity, diabetes, future cardiovascular disease, and tooth decay, just to name a few. According to the Centers for Disease Control and Prevention, SSBs intake is especially high among adolescent boys. Interestingly, adolescents who frequently drink SSBs also have more screen time on televisions, cell phones, computers, and video games. It's also been shown that adolescents whose parents drink SSBs daily are more likely to drink them regularly. This is another example of your health behaviors setting an example for your child's. You don't have to be perfect, but you do need to be aware.

Examples of SSBs:

- Regular soda (not sugar-free)
- Fruit juices that are not 100% fruit (check the ingredient list)
- Artificially flavored fruit drinks
- Sports drinks
- Energy drinks
- Some sweetened waters
- Flavored coffee and tea beverages (many options from fast-food coffee shops include a whole day's worth of added sugar)

Early adolescence is a great time to start healthy habits related to hydration. Because SSBs are often easily accessible outside of the home, consider not stocking them at home. Instead, explore a variety of other flavorful ways to consume beverages:

- Add a combo of fresh foods to a pitcher of water: cucumber slices + mint leaves; cucumber + citrus slices; fresh raspberries + lemon slices; fresh blackberries + strawberries + raspberries.
- Freeze fruit in ice trays to add to water.

The Scoop on Sports Drinks

Sports drinks were developed to replenish an athlete's energy and electrolytes during intense physical activity that lasted more than an hour. Nowadays, sports drinks are often marketed and commonly used as a daily drink, regardless of activity level. When consumed in this way, they add an unnecessarily high amount of added sugar, while also lacking nutrients. The American Academy of Pediatrics recommends that children and adolescents restrict or completely avoid regular intake of sports drinks, unless rapid carbohydrate replenishment is needed before, during, or after intense physical activity.

A few more tips:

- Plain water, along with naturally occurring electrolytes from a balanced diet, is the recommended hydration source for people 12 years of age, unless told otherwise by your pediatrician.
- Coconut water alone provides some electrolytes. Coconut water beverages may be a good option to use for hydration variety.
- Be aware of artificial sweeteners in "light" or "sugar-free" versions of sports drinks. While they will contain lower sugar content than regular sports drinks, there is **no amount**

of artificial sweeteners that is recommended as safe for children or adolescents to consume. The amount of artificial sweetener in products is not required on the nutrition label, so it's impossible to know how much is in each product. Some research has also shown a correlation between artificial sweetener intake and increased cravings for sugar.

- The recommended amount of added sugar per day is **less than 25 grams** (6 teaspoons)!

- The amount of added sugar a food product contains is required on the nutrition label. Check all labels to see how many grams of added sugar the product contains. Common food items with added sugar include sweetened beverages, yogurt, peanut butter, sauces/dressings, granola, protein bars, dairy and non-dairy milk, and breakfast products. (A 20-ounce bottle of soda can contain more than 16 teaspoons of added sugar!)

- In general, a good goal is to limit products with added sugar and use those that contain 3 grams of added sugar or less when necessary.

Closing Advice

It's natural to want nutrition advice to be written in stone: yes or no…all or nothing…"eat this, don't eat that." But getting it that way is unusual for any age category—including 12-year-olds. Each kid is different. So, use the general guidelines for amounts and types of foods listed for you, while continuing to encourage awareness and mind-body connection. You can do this by keeping an open mind when it comes to food for your child and yourself. Stay positive to avoid sparking feelings of shame related to food. Guide them in the exploration of their food preferences and mindset, even if that means trying new recipes together that end with a good laugh and throwing a frozen pizza in the oven!

> **Conversation Starters**
>
> - How do you feel about _____ (insert any change happening to their routine; eating a certain food; new school lunch schedule; energy when playing a sport)?
> - What food options do you have at your school lunch? Which ones do you like?
> - Do you feel hungry when you're in class?
> - Do you feel like you have enough to eat while you're at lunch, or are you rushing through it and still hungry after?
> - Do you ever feel tired or groggy during the school day? When?
> - What are your favorite meals? Favorite snack foods?

Chapter 4
THE NUTS AND BOLTS OF TWEEN SLEEP

How to help your child sleep better

Tyish Hall Brown, PhD, MHS
Director of Behavioral Sleep Medicine, Children's National Hospital

Most new parents are obsessed with their babies' sleep—when they do it, where they do it, how long they do it. They notice how sleep is tied to babies' moods (and to their own!) and ponder endlessly how best to facilitate healthy sleep habits. But at some point—certainly once a child is able to "take over" bedtime on their own—sleep gets short shrift in their minds. But should it?

As it turns out, despite the critical role that sleep plays in our kids' physical, psychological, social, and academic well-being, sleep problems are common among teens and tweens. The Centers for Disease Control and Prevention estimates that only 4 in 10 middle schoolers are getting the recommended 9 to 12 hours of sleep they need, with most kids extending their sleep on weekends in efforts to compensate.

Although there is still a lot that we do not know regarding the "why" of sleep, we do know that poor sleep has been linked to decrements in cognitive function, increased risk-taking, common mental health conditions, and poor overall health in tweens and teens. And we know that this lack of sleep or poor-quality sleep can be attributed to any number of clinical disorders and environmental influences. Here, we'll explore the various challenges 12-year-olds face in obtaining adequate sleep, as well as basic tips to help your tween improve their overall sleep health.

Sleep Disturbances in Tweens

When it comes to sleep disorders among tweens, **insomnia** is the most common—with prevalence rates as high as 40 percent in some studies. Insomnia is characterized by difficulty falling asleep, difficulty staying asleep, early morning awakenings, and/or poor sleep quality. Often, these difficulties arise because of changes in routine, new/exciting events, bad habits, or environmental factors. For example, a tween may experience difficulty falling asleep each night because their room is uncomfortably hot or cold, making it hard to settle comfortably in their beds. In our lifetimes, most of us will experience a few nights of insomnia. However, when insomnia is persistent—occurring three or more nights per week, lasting for at least one month—it becomes a more serious problem that requires professional attention.

For some 12-year-olds, inadequate sleep can be linked to **changes in circadian rhythms.** Puberty is a developmental time when our sleep/wake cycle naturally shifts, allowing tweens and teens to stay up later at night and wake up later in the morning. Although most teens can adapt to this physiological change, about 10 percent of teens will experience a phase shift delay that results in daytime impairment. Other teens may temporarily struggle with this transition because it is at odds with the demands of middle school life. Early school start times often require tweens to truncate their sleep, leaving too many children tired throughout the day. So, if your tween is going to bed at midnight and rising at 6 a.m. for school, they are persistently experiencing a sleep loss of about three hours.

Sleep and mental health are intimately connected in tweens. At a basic level, we know that their moods and frustration tolerance are affected by sleep loss. They may find it more difficult to deal with siblings or regulate their responses to emotionally charged situations when they are running low on sleep. However, drastic changes in sleeping habits often serve as an indicator or a warning sign for parents to check in with their tween to determine if professional help may be needed. For example, excessive sleepiness, short sleep (sleeping less than six hours at night), and nightmares are often attributed to mental health conditions such as depression, anxiety, bipolar disorder, and post-traumatic stress. Conversely, if a tween has been diagnosed with a mental health disorder, poor sleeping habits can often exacerbate the condition.

Although not common, it should be noted that some tweens suffer from **obstructive sleep apnea.** This is a serious condition that has been linked to an increased risk of metabolic disorder and mortality. If you hear your tween snoring loudly while they sleep with pauses in breathing or periodic gasps for breath, they may have obstructive sleep apnea. Many tweens with this disorder will experience poor quality sleep, daytime sleepiness, and sore throats upon awakening. Tweens who have enlarged tonsils, who are obese, or who have craniofacial abnormalities are more likely to develop this condition.

Sleep Disruptors in Tweens

There are a number of environmental and social factors that can negatively influence tween sleep. Although it is not likely that families can eliminate these factors altogether, this is where parents and their tweens can make the biggest difference.

- **Electronics:** Parents of middle schoolers will not be surprised to learn that smartphones, tablets, and computers can have a negative impact on sleep. The blue light emitted from electronic devices prevents the release of melatonin, a hormone that facilitates our transition into sleep, making it difficult to settle at night. Tweens should turn off all electronic devices at least 30 minutes (and ideally an hour) before bedtime. If this feels daunting, you're not alone. In keeping with behavioral principles, if you take away something, it's best to replace it with something equally engaging. Parents can brainstorm with their tweens to figure out what they might replace screen time with in their nighttime routine. Coloring, reading, and listening to music are all great examples of relaxing and non-activating pre-sleep activities.

- **Academic demands:** Academic demands can be difficult to balance for 12-year-olds. As your tween transitions from elementary to middle school, you may notice that their homework load has increased, along with teacher expectations, peer influences, and extracurricular activities. Many tweens find themselves staying up late to accommodate these competing demands, leading to chronic sleep loss.

- **Sports:** Although sports and activities can be a true boost to tween daily function and overall health, mismanagement of time can lead to sleep loss. Sports can be demanding, particularly if your child aspires to play their sport at elite levels. As a result, many tweens must manage the challenges of early/late practices, the stress of competition, and physical strains or injuries on top of their normal load.

- **Daytime naps:** Napping can negatively impact the ability to fall asleep and stay asleep. When tweens are overtired, they often want to nap during the day. But if your tween takes a midday nap, they awaken with a reduced sleep need, which has to build up again before they can fall asleep at night. It is recommended that tweens abstain from napping, particularly if they are having trouble falling asleep at night.

- **Stress:** Between balancing academic and social demands and living up to the often unreasonable expectations they have for themselves, tweens can feel as if the weight of the world is on their shoulders. This stress can manifest as somatic complaints, such as stomachaches or headaches, or it could impinge upon their sleep. Stress is often connected to insomnia complaints, such as difficulty falling and staying asleep.

- **Nighttime fears:** Often brought on by stress, fears may come in the form of worries about personal safety or even worries about dream content. While nighttime fears are far more prevalent in elementary-age children than in tweens, exposure to trauma may cause nighttime fears to linger and can be addressed with the help of a professional.

- **Food and drink:** What and when kids eat can be disruptive to their ability to obtain optimal sleep. Sugary foods and caffeine can make it hard to settle at night. A heavy meal within an hour of bedtime can also lead to disrupted sleep, as the body tries to digest and settle at the same time. Drinking liquids right before bedtime can cause nighttime awakenings, as kids will feel more compelled to use the bathroom during the night.

Building Healthier Habits

Your tween's sleep is governed by two processes that span a 24-hour sleep/wake cycle. The first process is based on environmental cues that alert their bodies that it is time for sleep. For example, the simple change from day to night signals internal mechanisms to start preparing for sleep, which is why daylight saving time shifts make people so tired. The second process is based on sleep need. When your teen wakes up in the morning, their need for sleep is low. As the day progresses, however, their sleep need builds, reaching its peak at night around the same time the environmental cues come into play.

There are some things your tween can do during the day to support their sleep/wake cycle and promote optimal sleep. **Regular exercise and activity** have been shown to promote better sleep by lowering stress levels and providing an outlet for extra energy. Just remember that earlier is better: When exercise is done within an hour of bedtime, it can be activating, making it difficult for tweens to settle into sleep.

A second factor that promotes optimal sleep is **sleep environment.** Light, noise level, temperature, and bedding all influence sleep. Some tweens may like their room pitch black, so blackout curtains can be helpful. Others prefer the presence of some light source, though any lights should be dim, and tweens should stay away from using brightly colored LED strip lights such as those commonly used to outline ceilings. If noise is an issue—either from outside or inside the home—then nature sounds and white noise machines can be a relaxing alternative. Some may even prefer music or an audiobook; just make sure that their choices are calming as opposed to stimulating. When it comes to temperature, around 65 degrees Farenheit, with comfortable bedding and blankets, is usually ideal. Also be sure to think about bedding and pajamas when assessing environmental factors.

The third sleep-promoting factor that is often overlooked is **consistency.** Our bodies respond best when we implement consistent routines and habits. The American Academy of Sleep Medicine recommends that children ages 6 through 12 obtain 9 to 12 hours of sleep per day. Based on your tween's sleep need, you can calculate the best bedtime by identifying a rise time and working backward.

Bedtime routines—which should typically last 30 minutes to an hour—should be thought of as activities that help your tween transition into sleep. These routines can include steps of basic personal hygiene, such as brushing teeth and taking a shower, as well as relaxing activities like journaling or meditation. Although the steps of a routine should be consistent, the relaxing activity can vary by night.

The last habit to encourage is **using beds only for sleeping.** It is human nature to create associations between our environment and activities, and sleep is no different. When tweens do their homework, talk on the phone, watch TV, or play video games in their beds, their bodies may begin to associate their beds with stimulating activities. This does not mean that tweens must stop those other activities, but it does mean they may need help identifying additional spaces they might use for these activities, whether it be in their room or in common areas.

How Parents Can Help

Understanding how sleep works and the barriers tweens face can help you support positive sleep health in your tween. Here is some additional advice.

1. Prioritize sleep. Most people think of sleep as a passive process, something that just happens. But with extremely busy schedules, tweens and their families need to take time to schedule in sleep. It's a good idea to sit down with your tween before the start of school and go over their daily schedule, as well as address the various things that might impede your child's sleep. For example, help make their environment comfortable *for them*. Consider a bedroom makeover—ensuring that bed, linens, lighting, noise levels, and temperature are conducive to great sleep. When parents model good habits and make sleep a family endeavor, tweens are more likely to engage in good habits themselves. And don't be afraid to offer words of encouragement when they do get to bed on time or wake up on time. This is still a learning process for them, and positive reinforcement helps.

2. Provide healthy food. You may not be able to control everything your tween eats, but you can control what is available to eat in your home. Instead of buying junk food and candy for snacks, try to include healthy options such as fruits, vegetables, cheeses, and natural popcorn. Try to provide balanced meals that include the four food groups (see the previous chapter for more guidance). Finally, be aware of the timing of their meals, and try to make dinner early enough in the evening to allow them to finish eating at least an hour before bedtime.

3. Establish a consistent bedtime. Despite their desire for independence, tweens are still growing and developing and require structure. Some parents unilaterally pick a bedtime for their tween and expect their tween to abide by it; other families discuss the merits of various bedtime options with their child to create better buy-in. Whichever method you choose, the key is to support your tween in meeting their bedtime goals as consistently as possible in order to foster optimal sleep. This could include helping them create a bedtime routine that is manageable and realistic and incorporating alarms to indicate when to start and stop various components of their nightly routine.

4. Promote independence. As with most aspects of this developmental period, parents can help by providing tools that facilitate a transition to independent sleep routines. Provide education around the importance of sleep, how it can impact our ability to function throughout the day, and how the persistent lack of adequate sleep can be detrimental to our health. Share the "why" of it all and point out how sleep challenges might hinder the ability to participate in tween things like sleepovers or school trips.

5. Address sleep health concerns. If you think that your tween has a sleep disturbance that is affecting their ability to function, seek professional help. There are sleep centers across the country that specialize in the treatment of pediatric sleep disorders. These centers are located in hospitals, academic institutions, or freestanding clinics. Professionals from the fields of psychology, pulmonology, pediatrics, and nursing often work together to provide a comprehensive approach to supporting sleep health. Professional societies, such as the National Sleep Foundation and the American Academy of Sleep Medicine, will often have lists of providers and their areas of specialty.

Closing Advice

There is undeniable relief in watching our kids grow from young children who need constant bedtime support to tweens and teens who are more than capable of making and following their own sleep routines. But be sure not to hand over those reins too fast; your tween still needs support. Once they have established their routine, check in with them periodically to see how things are going. Help them brainstorm ways to overcome any obstacles they may be facing. Try to avoid making bedtime contentious. Your tween is building habits that will serve as a foundation for their success moving forward. Helping them to prioritize sleep now will serve them for the rest of their lives.

Conversation Starters

- How many hours of sleep do you think 12-year-olds need each night? Do you think that you are getting that amount of sleep?
- Are there things that make it hard for you to fall asleep at night?
- What do you think is a fair bedtime? Thinking about when you need to wake up each morning, do you think this will allow you to get 8 or 9 hours of sleep each night?
- I noticed that you have been tired during the day lately; are you having trouble sleeping?

Chapter 5
THE IMPORTANCE OF MOVEMENT

How to encourage physical activity in a media-saturated world

Wesley O'Brien, PhD
School of Education, Physical Education, Sports Studies and Arts Programme, University College Cork

Zeinab Khodaverdi
Department of Biobehavioral Studies, Teachers College, Columbia University

Lots of things prevent 12-year-olds from actively moving their bodies around: lack of space, time, knowledge, and motivation, not to mention the powerful allure of social media and online gaming. Yet, just as a house built on a strong foundation is better able to stay standing for centuries, a child who is physically active is in a far better position to weather the many storms of life—physical, cognitive, social, and emotional.

Indeed, study after study shows that regular physical movement helps solidify the body's strength and resilience, enhances concentration, and boosts our overall well-being. Nurturing various kinds of movement in young people—ideally 60 minutes or more a day—can provide a powerful alternative to screen time, while also helping our youngsters navigate the challenges of a media-saturated world.

For 12-year-olds, who are at a critical juncture as they transition into early adolescence, active movement is highly influenced by the provision of tools (sports equipment, local amenities) and resources (green space, active role models) specific to the child's interests and abilities. The simple presence of a basketball can transform a child's video-gaming afternoon into a carnival of movement. Not only are throwing and dribbling fun, but these skills also improve coordination and physical strength, while also teaching invaluable lessons about timing, strategy, and teamwork. Such skills and learning can even transfer over to the 12-year-old's academic and social life, enriching their development in terms of character, mental health, and personal growth.

The Fundamentals of Movement

When kids engage in regular physical activities, they are engaging with three types of movement, or fundamental movement skills (FMS): locomotor, stability, and manipulative skills.

- Locomotor skills include running, jumping, hopping, and swimming. These skills become more sophisticated in activities like soccer, basketball, track and field events, and competitive swimming.
- Stability skills include balancing, twisting, and landing. They come into play during simple playground activities

like climbing or maintaining balance on a seesaw and in yoga, gymnastics, and martial arts.

- Manipulative skills involve controlling objects through actions, such as catching, throwing, kicking, or striking. These skills can be seen in sports like baseball, basketball, volleyball, and in activities such as juggling or playing a musical instrument.

While physical activity involves any bodily movement resulting in energy expenditure (e.g., increased heartbeat, harder breathing), FMS are the basic observable patterns of movement for adolescents. They include running in a straight line, balancing on one foot, and catching a tennis ball with one or two hands. You can see these building blocks of movement when your 12-year-old uses their larger muscle groups in pursuits such as sports and play.

Unlike general physical activity for adolescents, which should be experienced every day for at least 60 minutes a day, the promotion of FMS offers a slightly different focus. Here are our recommendations regarding the ideal frequency, intensity, length, and type of FMS that should be folded into their 60 minutes a day of physical activity.

1. **Frequency:** Encourage your adolescent to practice FMS at least twice a week.

2. **Intensity:** Encourage your adolescent to practice FMS while their heart rate is beating faster than normal (they will find it difficult to talk while practicing FMS).

3. **Length:** Ideally, adolescents will spend between 30 and 60 minutes a week engaging in FMS activities. To see changes in FMS competence, we recommend that children practice these movements for at least 10 weeks.

4. **Type:** Practice FMS in structured and unstructured environments. Structure refers to games and sports involving rules and regulations, such as organized soccer matches or dance classes, which give adolescents clear guidelines to follow and specific skills to develop. Unstructured movement is less regulated or planned, encouraging adolescents to explore their abilities through free play.

A friendly game of basketball or soccer not only promotes running and jumping (locomotion), but the game also requires planning and teamwork. A table tennis match can enhance hand-eye coordination and reaction speed (manipulative skills). A yoga challenge or a balance beam activity in the park can promote stability skills, which further encourages 12-year-olds to maintain balance in various poses while moving. Each of these activities provides an opportunity for your adolescent to continue to develop and refine their FMS while having fun.

The Barriers to Movement

Several things prevent today's adolescents from moving:

- Kids have an increased dependence on mobile device usage, video games, and TV. Such screen-based activities often replace the time that would have been spent in active play or sports.
- Many kids live in places where playgrounds and parks are sparse, overcrowded, or poorly maintained.
- Families with limited resources might not be able to afford sports equipment for their adolescents, or they might not be able to pay the membership fees within certain sports programs.

- Societal beliefs also play a crucial role in shaping the types of physical activities considered appropriate for children. For example, some misguided ideas label certain sports or physical activities unsuitable for girls, creating a barrier to participation and hindering potential positive impacts. These barriers, underpinned by societal norms and sometimes socioeconomic factors, are a global reality, and they curtail the ability of numerous children to develop their foundational and fundamental movement skills.

How Parents Can Get Adolescents Moving

There is no magic potion that can transform your 12-year old's physical habits. But a little opportunity and motivation can go a long way. Here are some ways to encourage your adolescent to move their body.

- **Use "personal bests."** Many adolescents (though not all) are inspired by their personal best targets. These targets are not meant to be compared to peers; these targets are specific to the individual only. For example, you might challenge your adolescent to see how many times in a row they can catch a tennis ball bounced off a wall without dropping it. While the distance from the wall is specific to the individual child, such a challenge is both fun and useful in mastering object control skills.

- **Accept a little risk.** While some activities may involve a certain level of risk, they are essential for adolescents to test their limits, learn about their capabilities, and develop a sense of autonomy. For instance, an adolescent might challenge themselves to climb a little higher on the playground jungle gym or try a new trick on their skateboard. Let them. Adolescents need to engage in such exploration, with appropriate supervision and safety measures, to foster their independence and confidence in what their bodies can do.

- **Be a role model.** Model an active lifestyle, not only by participating in physical activities with your 12-year-old, but also by embodying these values in your personal habits. This could be demonstrated by regularly going for a morning run, attending a weekly yoga class, or engaging in a hobby that requires physical activity, like gardening or cycling. By maintaining and showcasing your own active lifestyle, you instill in your adolescent the value of regular physical activity, motivating them to adopt similar habits.

- **Engage in activities that kids find enjoyable and challenging.** Join your adolescent for a basketball shoot-around to develop their catching, throwing, and shooting skills. Engage in a friendly tennis match to enhance their hand-eye coordination and striking skills. Play a game of tag, enhancing their running and dodging skills, or set up a simple obstacle course in your backyard that could incorporate various skills like hopping, crawling, and balancing. To develop flexibility and balance, try a beginner's yoga sequence together. This shared experience of movement with your 12-year-old reinforces the values of family time, togetherness, health, and well-being.

- **Get outdoors.** Go on a family hike. If time or distance limits that, encourage them to create a pre-planned outdoor route (such as a makeshift track using cones) with their friends or siblings. They can have a catch, play sports, or make up their own games. Another fun thing to do outdoors is to set up a safe and robust slackline for adolescents—an activity that also increases their stability.

- **Transform your living room into a playground.** If you have a valuable-free section, create a fun game of bouncing balloons or Nerf balls back and forth, challenging your adolescent to keep them in the air for as long as possible—an activity that enhances hand-eye coordination and reaction time. Or turn the middle of the room into a mini dance floor where your child can dance to their favorite songs, improving their rhythm and body coordination. You can also create a quiet yoga zone, allowing your adolescent to practice different poses, enhancing their balance and flexibility. These setups not only promote a variety of FMS, but they also provide a range of activities that your 12-year-old might find engaging and enjoyable.
- **Make time for free play.** When out and about, give yourself extra time and flexibility to allow for some free play. Give your child time to climb trees, run down hills, or crawl into tight spaces. These activities are not only good for their heart and spirit, but they also build body control, locomotion, and stability skills.

If you can consciously create an environment that facilitates physical activity for your adolescent, you are equipping them with skills that extend far beyond the physical health benefits. Although many things contribute to an adolescent's level of physical activity, you are a key player. But, while every minute of movement counts for 12-year-olds, it is important to remember that the amount of activity will naturally fluctuate from day to day. Some days, your adolescent will be more active, while on others, they will be less inclined to engage in physical activities. This is normal and not a cause for concern. It is the overall trend toward regular activity that matters, not the day-to-day variances. Over time, these active habits will contribute to an adolescent's overall health and development.

Closing Advice

Encourage your 12-year-old to participate in movements that are enjoyable, varied, and developmentally appropriate for their age and ability. Movement needs to occur across many different domains, such as in the home during leisure time, or in the school environment during physical education and sport.

Whenever possible, try to avoid being a technology warden. In other words, use technology, if available, to promote movement with your child, like movement-related apps or wearable devices. Let your 12-year-old become inspired through real-time movement data.

Integrate movement breaks at home. For example, every 30 minutes during homework or TV viewing, encourage everyone in the room to stand up and reach for the ceiling for 60 seconds.

Regardless of your physical activity background, be an active role model for daily movement. Let your 12-year-old experience different movements with you. Make time as a family to move and have really good fun along the way. Every weekend, see if you can dedicate at least one hour to visit a local park, beach, or hiking trail together—a place where movement is a necessity.

Finally, and most importantly, place true value on your 12-year-old moving every day. They may not love it at the moment, but when the storms of life begin to blow their way, they will thank you.

Conversation Starters

- Do you have any idea how much you should be moving in a week? Do you want to investigate the wearable devices and apps we can use to track it?
- Have you ever thought about trying gymnastics, dance, or maybe joining a sports team?
- When do you feel like moving the most? Is it morning, afternoon, or in the evening?
- Can you think of some fun ways to get moving inside the house when the weather is bad?
- What outdoor activities do you enjoy the most in our neighborhood?
- Are there any things that worry you about playing outside, either on your own or with your buddies?
- What outdoor family activities should we try together?

Chapter 6
CREATIVITY

How to lay the groundwork for innovation

Craig Balfany
Registered and Board-Certified Art Therapist,
Licensed Professional Counselor

Adolescence is a time of rapid neurodevelopmental change, including a heightened capacity for abstract thought, objectivity, and independence. It's also a period when children adjust their identities to suit the broader world and take new risks. Although these changes can bring challenges and confusion (for both parents and kids), there is cause to celebrate: It is from these changes that true, meaningful creativity is born. As it turns out, the 12-year-old brain is primed for innovation.

What Is Creativity?

Creativity is the generation of unique, unexpected, and compelling ideas. It is a blend of originality and usefulness defined within a particular context. While very young children are certainly imaginative, creativity requires thinking critically, finding hidden patterns, making new connections, and coming up with inventive solutions. Creative ideas are often generated when one lets go of what is *known* and is open to what is *possible*.

Initially, innovative ideas may appear irrational, yet they contain seeds that grow into valuable solutions. Individuals can be inventive in many aspects of their lives. Resourcefulness in generating new ideas is not an isolated act. Still, it depends on an individual's engagement in the socio-material world. Creativity is always relational, demonstrated by a connection between the individual, their culture, and their community. It is in these contexts that their creative vision can be verified and validated.

Stages of Creativity

In 1926, British psychologist Graham Wallas broke down the creative process into four stages which are still useful today.

Stage 1: Preparation

The preparation stage involves the preliminary work of generating ideas, doing research, gathering materials, and preparing the space.

Stage 2: Incubation

The incubation stage is when the mind feels safe to wander. It is the stage when one "sleeps on it," where ideas and concepts consolidate into the foundations for emerging products and solutions.

Stage 3: Illumination

In the illumination stage, the individual or group experiences a breakthrough and begins to see the solution to the problem. It is the "aha" moment.

Stage 4: Verification

The verification stage allows for refinement to the solution. During this stage, the innovator can go back into the incubation and illumination stages to further refine their idea and validate its usefulness.

Although these stages can be helpful, creativity is not linear. Your 12-year-old can flow forward and regress repeatedly in their journey to find creative solutions to their unique challenges and dilemmas. Studies have shown that there can be slumps or jumps in creativity associated with the different stages of child development, particularly in the transition from elementary to middle school. So please do not become discouraged if there is a downturn in your child's creativity from time to time.

Creativity and Self-Identity

A child moving into middle school will face new routines and expectations and different levels of structure. They are experiencing physical, cognitive, social, and emotional changes, and they begin to consider others' points of view and feelings. They start to understand cause and effect and may have an emerging openness to new experiences. Parents who can guide creative thinking in their children will allow them to connect the information in new and meaningful ways, which is humankind's most valuable skill.

Creativity is inherent in all individuals. It often emerges in early adolescence and continues throughout a person's life, facilitating the development of skills such as the pursuit of personal expression, lifelong leisure activities, and problem-solving approaches. Creativity conveys an individual's unique qualities. Parental support and encouragement benefits creative development and a positive self-identity.

8 Ways to Nurture Your Kids' Creativity

According to the theories of Alfred Adler, a physician and psychotherapist, all children possess their own "creative power," which is a synthesis of intelligence and imagination that helps guide their movement in life to overcome obstacles. Parents can nurture this creative capacity in many ways.

1. **Help kids discover what excites them.**

   Individuals who excel in creative pursuits are almost always genuinely excited about their work. Encourage your 12-year-old to name what motivates and excites them. If they struggle with this or respond with "I don't know," you can list some of your child's strengths and skills. For example, you could say, "You have artistic or musical skills," "You are a good problem solver," or "You are courageous." Acknowledging these strengths with your 12-year-old can be affirming of their developing creative interests.

2. **Let kids solve their problems and make their own decisions.**

   Sometimes we think of creativity in terms of artwork and stories, but it encompasses so much more than that, and it all starts with problem-solving. By providing 12-year-olds with opportunities to think about innovative solutions to problems, they can begin to integrate and apply what they are learning in real time. Encouraging kids to be curious, raise questions, and brainstorm solutions to challenges, such as school assignments or interpersonal conflicts, will help them develop out-of-the-box solutions.

3. **Welcome all ideas—even the unrealistic ones.**

   Even if an idea seems unrealistic and overly ambitious, supporting and celebrating your child's ability to generate new ideas will help ensure they are open to alternatives. When you are receptive to these ideas, it encourages creative thinking. It provides an opportunity for your 12-year-old to practice critical thinking as they evaluate the merits of their ideas.

4. **Assure kids that success is not the point.**

   Help your 12-year-old by telling them about barriers you have faced while trying to express your creativity. These barriers could be a lack of financial or material resources or being discouraged by others or one's inner critic. Sharing experiences can help reassure your child that they are not alone in confronting obstacles. When your 12-year-old attempts to overcome challenges, demonstrate encouragement by acknowledging the endeavor, whether the effort was successful or not.

5. **Tolerate mistakes and risk-taking.**

   Not all creative ideas are successful solutions. Your 12-year-old may make mistakes, or their solution may not fit the problem. Although this can be frustrating, teach your child to take responsibility for their successes and failures. A child who tends to blame others or themselves for mistakes misses out on learning from that experience. If your 12-year-old struggles with perfectionism, remind them of this quote by artist Salvador Dalí: "Have no fear of perfection—you will never make it."

   Challenging the norms and taking risks is part of the 12-year-old experience. Fortunately, all this risk-taking is what drives innovation in the creative process. Resourceful youth are willing to incur sensible risks and produce new ideas. Encourage them to try out for a role in a school play, perform a musical solo, or submit work for an art exhibit or poetry publication. Supporting these risks can help your child overcome self-doubt and build self-confidence. Discuss the consequences, challenges, and benefits of risk-taking on creative development. Reinforce the importance of resilience and frustration tolerance when pursuing creative endeavors. Projects may take longer than anticipated, performances may not go well, or others may not be satisfied with the results.

Taking the creative path can be a challenging journey filled with self-doubt and feelings that no one values what you are doing. To support your 12-year-old's self-efficacy, remind them of the value of their creative efforts. Twelve-year-olds must believe in themselves and their potential. Effective feedback neither over-encourages nor under-encourages their creativity.

6. **Collaborate!**

You can show your child how to be resourceful by collaborating in creative activities such as planning and preparing a meal, decorating a room, making art, or performing music together. These experiences allow your 12-year-old to share their ideas and be acknowledged for contributing. Innovative people often work with others in groups, and collaboration frequently produces creative work.

7. **Provide a creative environment.**

An environment that nurtures creativity and resourcefulness includes sharing your creative process and products with your child, including your frustrations and failures, to model what is involved in innovative activities. Providing stimulating and enriching activities is a highly effective way to increase creative potential. Integrating creativity into a child's schoolwork and social and leisure activities can motivate and reinforce knowledge and skills. Over time, your kid can incorporate these activities into their life and will gain knowledge and confidence, which can serve as a buffer against stress. Examples of hands-on and multisensory experiences include:

- Participating in visual arts activities like drawing, painting, clay work, sculpture, textiles, and photography, which provide opportunities to explore various materials. Each art medium has unique properties that can stimulate a 12-year-old on a continuum of sensory/kinesthetic, affective/perceptual, and cognitive/symbolic levels that promote curiosity and artistic expression.

- Practicing a visual art modality, which can be an excellent way to help your 12-year-old develop observational skills, focus their attention, organize their thoughts, and regulate emotions.

- Using simple art materials and having space to create, which can stimulate artistic engagement.

- Giving your 12-year-old a sketchbook to doodle and draw in, which helps to focus the mind and provides a sense of order and control when life feels chaotic. Even coloring books have benefits, as coloring provokes a similar physiological response in the brain as meditating. Coloring in patterns, particularly circular mandala forms, can be a stress- and anxiety-reducing activity.

- Playing an instrument, singing, recording beats, or writing lyrics, which all benefit creativity development. Researchers have found that musical training changes the brain structure and boosts engagement in the area responsible for decision-making. It can stimulate brain areas responsible for language development, speech perception, and reading skills. Music also acts as a medium to help process emotions and helps calm and reduce impulsivity.

- Engaging in dance and movement, which stimulate the psychological mechanisms of creativity that can arouse emotion and enhance the fluency of bodily movement. Dance and movement is an opportunity to be active, increase body awareness, and release pent-up energy but can also be an imaginative means of expression for children when they do not have the words to articulate feelings.
- Participating in theater or drama, which allows 12-year-olds to take risks to play new roles and characters. Opportunities to perform in front of others help them find their voice and build confidence and collaborative skills. Drama helps with perspective-taking and empathy-building, which are vital to executive functioning.
- Writing creatively, which can be focused on personal feelings, ideas, and experiences and dramatizes a constantly changing and developing inner sense of self and identity. Encourage creative writing by providing your 12-year-old with a writing journal, which can be a place to put down their thoughts, feelings, and observations that may be organized as stories, lyrics, or poems. The formal features of poetry provide a framework for experiencing a sense of order and organization. Poetry can integrate language, music, and imagery in a manageable way, most often with play, pleasure, and emotion. Writing and reading poetry can be a safe and creative way to explore and work through challenging emotions. To engage a 12-year-old in an inspiring writing exercise, have them imagine their best future self and write a story about that life as if it has already happened.
- Laughing and having a sense of humor, which have documented health benefits because they help reduce

stress. Participating in comedy and spontaneous improvisation using your imagination has been identified as a quick way to develop creative connections. Laughter can help your brain work better and stimulate originality by opening new, surprising concepts and ideas.

- Getting out in nature as often as possible, which enlivens all the senses. Feeling connected with the earth is inspiring and has been shown to reduce stress levels and increase relaxation. Twelve-year-olds are curious about the natural world around them. Presenting them with chances to explore the outdoors through recreation and environmental learning experiences lets them take a break, shift physical sensations, and supports productivity.

- Having access to and the use of resources (materials, technology, workspace, teachers, and mentors), which inspire innovative thinking is a crucial area that promotes creative growth.

Coming up with innovative insights takes time and effort. Provide time for your child to practice and develop skills. The repetition of skills helps to build new neural pathways in the brain and integrates learning. Allow your child's mind to wander and give them time and space for the incubation of creative thinking. Idle time may be perceived as wasted time or dawdling. Yet this time is needed to understand a problem, figure out how to address it, and then identify a solution. A 12-year-old engaged in the creative process may be required to work on projects for lengthy periods without an immediate reward. Remind your child about the benefits of delayed gratification by sharing your experiences and helping to apply these to their own lives.

Closing Advice

The brain of a 12-year-old is rapidly developing and is readily influenced by their familial, social, and educational environments. Inspiration can be enhanced by encouraging them to look at a subject and connect it with the broader social, cultural, and historical context. Use these opportunities to tap into your child's creative thinking to support this development. The creative path is an unfolding process that can allow 12-year-olds to begin to find themselves.

> **Conversation Starters**
>
> - What do you think about that excites you? Can you tell me about it or show me what you are working on?
> - What inspired you to come up with this idea?
> - What has been your biggest challenge or frustration with this project?
> - How could you use your creative skills to help you in other areas of your life?
> - How do you think your idea/project/performance turned out?
> - If it was unsuccessful, what might you do differently next time?
> - What might be the unintended consequences of your plan?
> - What do you hope to do or accomplish next?
> - Would you like some help?

Chapter 7
IDENTITY

How to support your adolescent's self-discovery

**Joanna Lee Williams, PhD, MSEd, and
Andrew C. Pool, PhD, MSc**

Among the many profound and exciting changes taking place as children enter adolescence is the process of self-discovery. Our 12-year-olds are figuring out who they are, which makes identity development an important aspect of early adolescence. Young people's identities are increasingly tied to choices they make about who they want to spend their time with, how they present themselves to others, and the activities and spaces they enjoy. At 12 years old, your tween is exquisitely sensitive to the information they receive from those around them. Family, friends, cultural and societal expectations, experiences at school, and messages in the media all play a part in how they view themselves.

Your tween may adjust their beliefs and behaviors based on feedback and may feel like they're one person at school and another at home.

Young adolescents are making sense of lots of different experiences, while also working to figure out who they are. A 12-year-old's identity is developed, in part, based on relationships and feedback received from others.

As young people move through adolescence and their brains continue to develop, their identity is also likely to change. Here are some questions that often accompany the early periods of identity exploration:

- *Who am I, separate from my family?* Young adolescents may want to express new and different identities separate from the ones they hold in their family.
- *How do I want others to see me?* Presenting oneself differently across spaces (e.g., school vs. home) requires young people to become more flexible and attuned to the cues they are receiving in various situations.
- *How do I fit in with my friends?* Finding a place with peers becomes increasingly important, and for some young people, navigating where they fit into the social landscape may take time and involve multiple changes.
- *How do I express my values while still having others like me?* Youth might think more about how to balance their own values with the opinions of others when making decisions and interacting with peers.
- *What am I good at? What do I enjoy?* Young adolescents are in the early stages of developing new passions and may lose interest in past hobbies as they gain new experiences.

These kinds of complex questions are surfacing during a period of profound change. Young adolescents' bodies and brains are changing rapidly. They may return to school after a summer break, only to find that they and their peers look completely different than before (think growth spurts, breast development, and new body hair).

Twelve-year-olds are becoming more sensitive to social information and are increasingly self-conscious. They may overestimate how much other people (especially their peers) are focused on them, and they are prone to misinterpreting social cues. They are also still learning how to regulate their responses to feedback. Connections in their brains are strengthening, especially in areas related to emotion, so emotional reactions, both positive and negative, may be really strong. Their cognitive skills are expanding, which means tweens are primed to learn new information and are thinking about themselves and the world in more abstract and nuanced ways. Twelve-year-olds are exploring new identities during a time of rapid physical, cognitive, and social-emotional growth, and the need for approval (again, especially from peers) can be amplified during periods of change.

How 12-Year-Olds Explore Their Identity

Working on identity may involve emulating behaviors of peer groups your tween hopes to join, or of other "influencers" they admire, like their favorite athlete, musician, TikToker, or YouTuber. While young adolescents are seeking places where they fit in, they often also want to stand out. Identity exploration can involve trying out new styles and asking for more control over personal decisions, from clothing and hairstyles to extracurricular activities and time spent with friends. They may question rules and test limits, which are all normative behaviors as youth are exploring their place in the world.

The process of identity exploration is a gradual one—it takes time and experience for us to have a solid sense of who we are. Yet, in early adolescence, changes in self-definition may seem abrupt or frequent. Sometimes tweens have experiences that create just enough conflict to get them thinking about their place in the world. These experiences may happen most frequently in peer settings, where tweens often communicate and regulate norms about what is considered appropriate or acceptable behavior. Seemingly minor questions from a peer about why your child has worn a particular outfit, why they speak a certain way, or why they like a style of music can spark reflection about how your child wants to be seen by others. Changes in behavior may follow, especially if your 12-year-old feels they need to act differently in order to fit in.

Twelve-year-olds may also be trying to understand themselves in relation to different aspects of identity—like their gender, religion, race, and sexuality. Young adolescents are in the early stages of creating a sense of self that feels consistent across different aspects of identity, in different contexts, and with different people. That is a tall order! Doing so while navigating physical, social, and emotional changes along with other new things (like the transition to middle or junior high school) can be overwhelming when you don't feel supported, heard, or understood.

Families as Foundations for Exploration

Early identities are deeply influenced by family experiences and traditions. Young people may find comfort in the ability to define some aspects of themselves with certainty, whether it be a faith-based identity or a multigenerational commitment to a beloved sports team. These identities may feel so solid that a young person never questions them and instead uses them as a source of stability as they consider other aspects of themselves that are less well-defined.

As 12-year-olds explore, they may be excited to share newfound knowledge with you. If they share something that you have already given deep consideration, remember that it is still new for them, and they may not be looking to you for answers. In fact, it is a good time for you to remind yourself that your child is an expert on their own life and their active search for answers to the question, "Who am I?" is helping them gain even more expertise. Your role is to be a sounding board. You supportively listen to their growing understandings and developing thoughts and guide them when needed.

Supporting Identity Development

How 12-year-olds see themselves is going to be shaped in part by how others—parents, peers, teachers, siblings—see them. They may also be influenced by how young people like them are portrayed in the media. For some, the range of "possible selves" seems endless. Others may be limited by lack of access to opportunities or by other people's stereotypes about expected outcomes. For example, tweens of Asian descent may feel boxed in by frequent portrayals of Asian youth who only care about math and science. Latinx youth may have to challenge peer or adult assumptions about their citizenship status or ability to speak English proficiently. Consistent support from parents empowers young adolescents as they envision themselves in the present and future.

As young adolescents process new experiences and dynamic physical, social, and emotional changes, parents can help by letting children know that finding ways to fit in and stand out and discovering new parts of oneself is normal and healthy. It is important to be open as tweens try out different presentations of themselves. Of course, being consistent with the rules and boundaries you've created to keep them safe still applies. Choices that involve risky behavior or that compromise morals require action, even if they are part of the identity exploration process. You don't want drinking, drug abuse, or unsafe sexual behavior to become an integral part of your tween's identity. If you suspect your tween is engaging in these behaviors, it's important to quickly intervene with your unwavering support and love. Guide them toward professional help, if needed. For more ideas on preventing risks, see Chapter 12: Risk-Taking.

Identity Development in a Diverse World

Young adolescents may start to spend time thinking about what it means for them to be a member of a particular racial, ethnic, or cultural group. This may be especially relevant for youth of color, as others often view them in racial terms. But white youth can also have experiences that cause them to think about what race means to them. Here are some questions that 12-year-olds may be asking about racial identity:

- *What is race and what does it mean to me? Do I have a racial identity?* Young adolescents may become more sensitive to experiences where race is made an issue; likewise, specific encounters (e.g., a comment by a peer, a post on social media) may prompt them to think more about their own race. Some youth may not have knowledge or experience to help them make sense of this information, especially if they have not had opportunities to learn or talk about race.

- *What are the racial-ethnic backgrounds of the people around me? How comfortable am I with difference?* Youth may increasingly become aware of race and racial group differences, especially if they make school transitions that expose them to peers from more diverse backgrounds. Of course, their awareness of racial differences and similarities may depend on how much their own racial-ethnic background matters to them.

- *Do my friends understand my racial-ethnic background? How much does that matter to me?* As social cliques become more prominent, friendships may change, and some youth may choose to spend more time with peers who share their racial or ethnic background. Youth who share a racial-ethnic background are still individuals with their own values, beliefs, and behaviors, but being around similar peers can feel like a safe place to share common experiences.

Parents and caregivers play an important role in supporting 12-year-olds as they explore their racial or ethnic identity. Age-appropriate books and media with authentic portrayals of diverse people and experiences can be helpful starting places for tweens and can provide an entry point for conversations between you and your child; just be mindful of sources that perpetuate stereotypes and generalizations, discussed in more detail below.

Early adolescence is an important time to foster a sense of cultural pride in teens and to challenge stereotypes about their own and other racial groups. If your family has important cultural traditions, explain and celebrate them. Help your 12-year-old learn about and value difference and diversity so they are prepared to engage with others who may view the world differently than they do.

In early adolescence, youth may become increasingly aware of stereotypes and realize that society frequently portrays some racial groups as heroes and leaders and others as victims, foreigners, or lawbreakers. Have open conversations with 12-year-olds about the harm in such stereotypes, and provide evidence to counter them. For example, if your tween determines that their new Spanish-speaking classmate must be from Mexico based only on assumptions, you have an opportunity to ask questions that prompt reflection, like, "Why do you think they're from Mexico?" and "How can you get to know more about your new classmate?" Stereotypical presentations in the media also offer opportunities for you to point out that people with shared ancestral heritage are not all the same and explain the harm in believing that they are. This encourages open-mindedness about the value of diversity and can inspire young people to stand up and push back when they witness or experience racial injustice. This work is particularly important during early adolescence, when young people need support to make sense of racism and other forms of oppression that may become increasingly more complex as they get older.

While instilling cultural pride is important, being realistic about the realities and consequences of racial stereotypes is another consideration. For instance, if you are a parent of a young adolescent from a group who may be disproportionately targeted by the police (e.g., Black, Latinx, and Native American), you may need to engage in conversations about what to do during a police encounter.

Promoting cultural pride, dispelling racial stereotypes, and preparing youth for encounters with bias can help support positive racial-ethnic identity development. There are also a couple of things you should not do. You should not avoid conversations about race with your child. While it may be an uncomfortable subject for you, especially if you have not had many chances to talk about race, it is important to create space to talk about it. Your 12-year-old may be more comfortable making mistakes with you or asking you questions than they will be in other circumstances. We should have the tough conversations in our homes precisely because they're tougher to have outside of them.

You should not encourage your young adolescent to be "color-blind." Yes, we are all human and share many commonalities. But the reality is that we live in a society where race matters. Recognizing and acknowledging race does not make you prejudiced or biased. It can be helpful to use specific terminology with your tween so they have access to appropriate vocabulary when they need it. For example, you can explain what "BIPOC" stands for or point out that "Asian-American" is a term that includes people from a diverse range of backgrounds. You can also acknowledge that terms and labels change over time, and that individuals may prefer specific ones (e.g., "White" or "European American"; "Native American" or "Indigenous"). Pretending differences do not exist may make it harder for 12-year-olds to engage in meaningful relationships with people from different backgrounds and to recognize instances of racial bias.

You know your child well, and they know themselves even better. At this moment, race, ethnicity, or culture may not be an important part of their identity. Athletics, hobbies, or academics may be more central to how they currently define themselves. This is normal and should be respected. We should not push children to make race a defining feature of how they see themselves. Instead, be prepared to engage in conversations when the topic of race comes up. Expose your child to people from different backgrounds and life experiences. Prepare them to recognize racial stereotypes and related injustices. As you do, your young adolescent will learn to develop a healthy sense of self, both broadly and within the context of their unique racial or cultural identities.

Online Identities

Social media provides a wealth of opportunity for young adolescents to create, test, and re-create various versions of themselves. Many youth use social media to stay in close contact with the same friends they have at school. Others use social media or gaming sites to tap into their creativity and imagine new, virtual identities. Some may go online to connect with peers who share similar interests in music, fashion, or other hobbies.

One challenge for parents is that digital technologies, particularly social media, are not often designed with young adolescents in mind. Many platforms require users to be at least 13 but do not have systems in place to verify a user's age. While debates abound about whether digital technology is good or bad for young adolescents (most experts agree it can amplify both positive and negative feelings), the reality is that its use is nearly ubiquitous among young adolescents, and digital technologies offer spaces for parents to support their 12-year-old's learning and help them make sense of the information they encounter online. Listen carefully when your tween tells you about something new they came across online. If it sounds fishy, ask follow-up questions about where they saw this information and if they think it's accurate. Know where and when your tween is active online (e.g., YouTube, TikTok, Instagram), but resist the urge to closely monitor their accounts and comment on every post. Intervene immediately to keep your tween safe if you become aware of risky or harmful behavior such as cyberbullying or sexting.

As young adolescents use online spaces to project themselves to friends and others, they may do so in a way that seems inconsistent or out of character with how you see them. The feedback they receive through their self-portrayals online is part of the process of identity development. Jumping to conclusions or interpreting their posts out of context may push your child to find ways to hide their online personas from you. If you're concerned, ask them to find out more about why they choose to present themselves in a particular way. (See the Conversation Starters at the end of this chapter for some examples of questions to ask.)

Overcoming Challenges

For some 12-year-olds, the process of identity exploration may be challenging. For those feeling like they don't know who they are or where they fit in, ask them how they feel when they're with different people or doing different activities. Ask when they feel most connected, disconnected, or comfortable. Telling young adolescents to just "be themselves" may not be helpful if they're struggling, but giving opportunities for self-reflection can create the space to start figuring out the answers on their own.

Of course, even if a young person appears to have a strong sense of self, sudden changes—starting a new school, moving to a different town, losing or gaining a family member—can leave them feeling like they don't know where they belong. Just as when you became a parent for the first time and had to figure out how your new role fit into your self-image, 12-year-olds need support to create a clear sense of self under new circumstances. Give them unconditional love as they adapt to their new surroundings. Check in with them to see how they are processing drastic changes. These can be excellent opportunities to build their resilience so they are better equipped for all of the uncertainties life can bring.

Even when our 12-year-olds don't yet feel good about themselves, it is critical they know we will love them just as they are. It is our stable presence and unwavering love that supports them so they can withstand challenges and offers them the security that allows them to find themselves.

Closing Advice

As 12-year-olds start building a sense of themselves and finding places where they feel most comfortable, it is critical that they have our support. This is especially true when they seem resistant or say they don't want it. We know that warm and responsive parenting helps to encourage identity development. Young adolescents who can navigate the terrain of possible identities and land in a space down the road where they can say, "This is who I am!" with confidence will have a strong, grounding foundation as they make increasingly complex and impactful decisions throughout adolescence and beyond.

Conversation Starters

- How do you think your close friends would describe you? How about your teachers?
- I noticed that you don't seem interested in [past hobby/activity] anymore. What are some new activities you might want to try?
- How does your social media activity reflect your interests and who you really are?
- What do you like most about your current group of friends?
- What do you have in common with your friends? How are you different from them?
- Which friends help you feel most comfortable, like you can be yourself?
- How important is it for you to feel like you fit in with your friends?
- In what ways do you behave differently with your friends than with your family? How about at school versus at home? How about online?
- What do you prefer to do with your friends instead of your family? What do you prefer to do with your family?
- Who do you like to connect with online? What do you like about the people you follow on social media?
- What would you do if one of your friends did something that you thought was not right?
- What would you say to your friends if they wanted you to do something you are not supposed to?

Chapter 8
FAMILY DYNAMICS

How to strengthen your
relationship with your child

Karissa DiMarzio, MS, and Justin Parent, PhD

Despite our best efforts, there is only so much we, as parents, can control. At the age of 12, your child is on the cusp of one of life's most important developmental transitions. Gone are the days of bedtime stories and kissing scraped knees; in their place arrives new discussions and challenges in which your child will begin to explore their growing desire for independence. For some parents, this transition can be extremely difficult to navigate, because much of the last decade has been spent picking children up when they fall, fending off invisible monsters, and offering endless assurances that everything will be fine. For others, no challenge will ever compare to that of the newborn and toddler phases, with 12 almost guaranteeing more sleep, freedom, and alone time for parents. Regardless of how you feel, the coming years will mark a clear shift in your relationship with your child, as well as in your approach to parenting. As with all things, there will be good days and there will be difficult days. But there are steps you can take now to reinforce your relationship in preparation for these formative years.

"Tell me and I forget, teach me and I remember, involve me and I learn." This Chinese proverb is an excellent representation of the shifts in learning that occur in adolescence. Prior to this point in your child's life, rule-setting tends to be easier and you are more likely to know and be involved in every aspect of your child's life, because younger children are more likely to ask for a parent's help when needed. Adolescence, on the other hand, is the beginning of a more hands-on approach to learning, where children begin experimenting with new things and people, branching out to learn lessons firsthand, and unfortunately, sometimes learning the hard way. In these next few pages, we provide an overview of some of the interpersonal challenges you can expect during this time, as well as advice on how you and your family can proceed.

Tell: Reinforce Love and Acceptance

Twelve-year-olds are often called "preteens" or "tweens," a description meant to capture their positioning as not-quite-children but also not-yet-teens. This "in-between" status means that, for some parents, this year may remain at a more innocent coming-of-age level of eventfulness, while for other parents, the intensity of independence may begin to heat up, with boundary-pushing beginning to occur and perhaps some minor rule-breaking. Either way, it is very unlikely that parents will observe the degree of rebellion and chaos stereotypically attributed to teenagers at this point (think popular but over-the-top movies and shows like *Thirteen*, *Shameless*, and *Euphoria*). What does underlie this entire spectrum of possible behaviors, however, is a shift in identity. For many children, this year will mark the beginning of significant hormonal changes, with 12 being in the average range of puberty onset for adolescents in the United States. See Chapter 1 for a deeper dive into puberty.

Everyone has an "awkward" phase. This phase and the increase in hair, acne, and body mass that accompanies it can take a real toll on your child's self-confidence. What can make a difference, however, is how you help your child navigate these changes. Open communication is key here. Many of the changes your child undergoes this year, and in the coming years, may or may not be something they know to expect or fully understand. In terms of your family dynamics, this may manifest as attempts to distance themselves from family in an effort to have more privacy. A family who normalizes this developmental process (e.g., openly discussing menstrual cycles rather than giving words like "period" and "pads" or "tampons" negative connotations or not mentioning them) sends the message that what children are experiencing and feeling may be uncomfortable but that *it is okay*. Given the additional peer pressure and relational problems that will come with wanting to fit in at school, as well as new feelings of physical attraction that may be beginning to develop, parental communication and warmth is important, but reinforcing your family's love and acceptance of your child is *essential*. There will be challenges to parent-child closeness in adolescence, and your family may spend less time together, but as your child figures out who they are and what they value, it will be the stability that your child relies on.

Teach: You Are Your Children's Model

The changes your child experiences during this time run the added and often dreaded risk of teen moodiness (we're picturing exasperated sighs, slamming doors, and eardrum-pounding angsty music). These displays may make you feel like nothing you do is making a difference, or that everything you say goes in one ear and out the other, but the reality is that your actions matter so much more in these moments. While it may seem like you and your child are increasingly at odds with one another, your child—whether they are aware of it or not—will continue to learn from you, specifically when it comes to handling all of the intense and difficult emotions that come with puberty. **Emotion socialization** (ES) is a term we use to describe the process in which children directly and indirectly learn how to express, understand, and regulate their emotions. In this respect, how *you* react to or manage emotions has a huge impact on how your *child* learns to react to and manage emotions. We provide a few examples of how this might play out in the table below.

Trigger	Parent Response	ES Reaction Type	Child Reaction(s)
Child nervously tells parent they plan to quit a school sport they both bonded over	Unsupportive Example		
	Tells child they are disappointed with them and withdraws from the child	Punitive: parent evokes guilt from the child and expresses disapproval by creating distance (i.e., giving the "cold shoulder")	Feels guilty for upsetting the parent, may change mind despite it not being what they really want in the situation; is less likely to open up in the future with similar concerns
	Supportive Example		
	Expresses understanding, mentions importance of extracurricular involvement, and problem-solves with child to come to a compromise (e.g., finish the season, replace with another activity)	Problem-focused: parent validates how child is feeling and ensures they feel heard; problem-solves with child to come to a compromise	Feels validated, is reassured that parent still loves and accepts them despite their decision; is more likely to be open with parent in the future with similar concerns

Trigger	Parent Response	ES Reaction Type	Child Reaction(s)
Child becomes angry and cries after sibling accidentally breaks one of their possessions	Unsupportive Example		
	Tells child it is not a big deal and to stop being a baby	Minimization: parent invalidates and devalues child's feelings	Views situation as unfair, perceives that other child is the "favorite"; feels sad and less emotionally close to parent, may learn to bottle up emotions rather than express them
	Supportive Example		
	Listens to child, expresses understanding, and explains that mistakes happen; helps child calm down through physical touch, deep breathing	Emotion-focused: parent validates how child is feeling, sends message that those feelings are okay and provides comfort	Is comforted, sees feelings acknowledged and valued by parent; learns to better regulate their own emotions over time

In the unsupportive examples, the parent's reaction can be emotionally confusing and potentially even harmful, because what is signaled to the child is that (1) the child's desire for autonomy is not as important as the parent's needs, and (2) anger and sadness are unacceptable emotions. In the supportive examples, however, the parent not only models appropriate regulation and coping skills, but the parent also acts in a way that lets the child know it is okay to express and talk about those emotions, emphasizing the parent-child relationship as a safe space. Once in a while, the unsupportive practices are likely inconsequential (everyone has bad days!), but on a regular basis, these responses can have a significant impact on a child's development, including, but not limited to, their emotion regulation and interpersonal skills. This can have a negative cascading effect in the dynamics of the family if the child feels less close to the parent and ultimately communicates less out of fear about anything as minor as a simple mistake to something more serious like risky sexual behavior or substance use later.

Emotions aren't the only aspect of family life and relational health that parents model for their children. The way you deal with conflict in the family is also important! Many parents try to hide conflict from their children, fearing it will damage them in some way. But healthy conflict resolution can be very good for children to observe, as it teaches them how to communicate during times of heightened emotions and how to navigate differences in relationships. The benefits of such modeling can transfer not only to the parent-child relationship, but also to the sibling relationship as well (though this one may take some extra discussion and mediation in the beginning). After all, the parent-child relationship will not be the only one that is impacted by the changes your child goes through this year and in the coming years. Siblings, too, may be feeling the changes in the family atmosphere that come with your child's growth. In the early years, siblings might have been reliable playmates. At 12, that may no longer be the case for your child. In most cases, this is no reason to panic, as sibling relationships will balance out again with time. Your child is simply branching outside the family to expand their support systems with similar-aged and more like-minded peers.

Involve: Learning-Focused Conversations with Your Child

This period of transition brings with it a host of new situations for parents to navigate. Prior to this point, your child may have taken a very active role in the family, participating in movie or game nights, attending family-centered events like birthday parties, or playing with siblings, all with little to no fight on their part. Now, you may begin to observe prioritization shifts from family time to alone time, siblings to friends, and so on. These are all healthy and developmentally expected shifts, and in the absence of any threats of harm to themselves (e.g., self-harm, substance use) or others (e.g., physical fights, bullying) often aren't cause for concern.* Your child is exploring their desire for autonomy and wanting to distinguish themselves as an individual. In order to do that, they will request more freedom and privacy. It is your call to determine what is appropriate based on your knowledge of your child, their needs, and their environment, but it is important to not stifle these attempts completely, as it could discourage open communication and honesty from your child. We recommend creating open dialogues with your child and involving them in discussions before making key decisions.

Although your child is still far from being considered a grown-up, they will want to be treated with more adult consideration. This might involve discussions about things like hanging out with friends outside the home, starting social media profiles, playing video games online with strangers, enforcing respect for privacy between siblings, wearing new styles of clothing, or starting to wear makeup. If you have more than one child, varying rules for each will surely present a headache at some point or another. Communication is key. "Because I told you so" or "Because I said so" rarely resolves a disagreement, but if you engage your child in a conversation about why you are making certain decisions and, as the situation calls for, allow them to be part of the decision-making, you should observe less upset. In this respect, parents of 12-year-olds may start noticing their relationship shift from that of just *parent*-child to also *advisor*-child. Parents do not have all the answers (we rarely do!), but that is the great part of open dialogues: They create space for learning not just for your child, but for you, too!

---

* If your child is showing signs of or engaging in any of these more serious behaviors, please contact emergency services, school officials, and/or other professionals in your child's life (e.g., pediatrician, therapist). Who you call will depend on the specific situation, but it is extremely important to do so as quickly as possible to ensure that you and your family receive the proper support and that all involved remain safe.

It can be very easy at this stage of your child's development to unintentionally slip into patterns of reactivity, where you both end up mostly speaking over each other and neither of you feel heard by the other. To avoid this, we recommend the following steps:

1. **Engage in active listening**, focusing on what your child is saying in the moment instead of what you would like to say or plan to say in response.

2. **Reflect back** what your child has said through paraphrasing and confirm that you have understood what your child intended to convey.

3. **Share your own feelings and perspectives** with statements like, "I feel _____ when you say _____" or "I understand you feel/think _____, but I _____."

4. **Work together** to come to a solution to the issue under discussion.

Closing Advice

Think of your family as the foundation of your child's development; reinforce that foundation not with critiques and judgment, but with affirmations and understanding. Put simply, *tell* your child you love them and make sure they don't forget; *teach* them by example, so what they pick up from you they always remember; and *involve* them in the discussions that pertain to them so they learn from and understand the reasons behind your expectations. By doing so, you will prepare your child for the future and position your family as a reliable, supportive structure your child can fall back on no matter what that future may bring.

Conversation Starters

- In an ideal situation, what would your family respecting your privacy look like for you?

- Let's discuss chores. You're getting older and your amount of homework is increasing, but your [dad/mom] and I still believe it's important for you to help out. What do you think would be a fair expectation right now?

- I don't feel comfortable with you doing X because of Y and Z. But I understand it is important for you to have this time with your friends. How can we approach this or change so that you are able to hang out with your friend(s) but we feel more comfortable?

- I know a lot of your friends are playing online, but I do not like the idea of your playing with strangers. I'd like to set up some parental controls to meet you halfway. What are your thoughts about this?

- What types of clothing are "in" right now? Do your friends wear makeup? What are your thoughts about that?

- I noticed you've been more conscious about what you're eating/how much exercise you're doing. What are your reasons for these changes?

Chapter 9
THE POWER OF FRIENDSHIP

How to help encourage positive peer relationships

Jonathan B. Santo, PhD
Department of Psychology, Adolescent Development, University of Nebraska, Omaha

You might be the first to notice in your child's early adolescence that peers are becoming increasingly important. There are some key points that you should know about the importance of peers during this time. Perhaps most importantly, peers play a vital role in social development. Children learn social skills and behaviors by interacting with their peers. During early adolescence, peers become particularly important in helping your child develop a sense of identity, learn social norms, and navigate social situations. The quality of these peer relationships can also impact your child's emotional well-being. Positive relationships can boost self-esteem, while negative ones can lead to anxiety, depression, and other emotional problems. Although there are a number of positive aspects of adolescent peer relations, there are difficulties as well, bullying among them, so parental involvement is important. Children are susceptible to peer pressure during early adolescence. You can play a key role in helping your child learn to resist negative peer influence and make positive choices.

Acceptance and the Importance of Being Liked

It's important to highlight how much your tween wants to be liked by their peers during this adolescent period. Here are some things you should know:

1. The need for peer acceptance is normal. Adolescents have a strong desire to fit in with their peers and be accepted by them, and this is part of the adolescent developmental process.

2. Peer acceptance can impact self-esteem. Adolescents who are accepted by their peers tend to have higher self-esteem and a positive self-image. Conversely, those who are rejected by their peers may experience lower self-esteem and a negative self-image.

3. Peer acceptance can influence behavior, for good and ill. Adolescents are more likely to engage in behaviors that are consistent with the norms of their peer group.

4. Parental support is still important. Adolescents who have supportive parents tend to have better mental health and social outcomes, even if they do not always feel accepted by their peers.

5. Parents should encourage tweens to participate in activities that align with their interests and values. Encouraging healthy communication and social skills can also help adolescents build positive friendships.

Friendships

Twelve is an age where friendships may change frequently, as teenagers explore new interests and social groups. It's important for you to support your child during these changes and help them navigate the ups and downs of friendship. If your child is feeling hurt by a comment that one or more of their friends made about an opinion they expressed, remind them that a true friend respects an opinion, interest, or choice no matter how different it may be from the group's. And the same is true the other way around. If another friend is being picked on for having a different thought, encourage your child to be sensitive and not just to go along with the group's opinion.

Quality matters more than quantity. The number of friends your child has is less important than the quality of those friendships. Encourage your child to focus on developing positive, healthy friendships with people who share their interests and values.

Friendships as a Framework for Intimacy Development

Adolescent friendships serve as a crucial way to build intimacy, which is an important aspect of social and emotional development. Intimacy can refer to emotional closeness, physical closeness, or a combination of both. Adolescents may experience intimacy in different ways, such as through romantic relationships, close friendships, or familial relationships. All serve as a normal part of development.

As with everything, communication is key: Encourage your child to communicate openly and honestly with their friends and romantic partners. Help them develop the skills to communicate their needs and boundaries and to respect the needs and boundaries of others. Model your own boundaries and be open about what you expect from good friends. Talk with them about their feelings and what others may be feeling in certain situations.

Healthy and respectful relationships are essential. You can encourage them to seek out friends who treat them with kindness, respect, and empathy. Your child may struggle with navigating the complexities of intimate relationships. Offer your child support and guidance and help them access resources, such as counseling or therapy, if needed.

Friendships as Protection from Negative Experiences

Intimate friendships can serve as buffers against the negative effects of difficult experiences. For one, peer relationships provide a source of emotional support. Adolescents who have supportive friends can rely on them during challenging times. This can help them feel less alone and more able to cope with stress and adversity. Their peers can also help demonstrate healthy coping strategies and provide optimism. Friends may encourage your child to seek help when they are struggling. This can be especially important when your child is hesitant to ask you or a teacher for help.

Ultimately, friends provide a sense of belonging. Adolescents who feel like they belong to a group of friends may experience less loneliness and social isolation. This sense of belonging can help them cope with difficult experiences and feel more connected to their community, and friends can encourage your child to try new activities or explore new places. This can help counterbalance the negative effects of difficult experiences and promote resilience. You can support your child by encouraging them to spend time with positive, supportive friends and by fostering an environment of open communication and support at home.

Concerns Around Peer Pressure

There are aspects of friendship that can also be of concern to parents, peer pressure among them. Peer pressure—the influence that peers have on an individual's behavior, thoughts, and feelings—is a common issue that many adolescents face. Your child may feel pressure from their peers to conform to certain behaviors or beliefs, even if they do not necessarily agree with them. It's worth pointing out that peer pressure can have both positive and negative effects. Positive peer pressure can encourage healthy behaviors, such as exercising or studying, while negative peer pressure can lead to risky or harmful behaviors, such as substance abuse or bullying.

Part of how your child navigates the challenges of peer pressure is through building their own independence. You can encourage your child to think for themselves and make their own decisions. Help them understand that it is okay to say no to their peers if they are uncomfortable with a situation or behavior. Of course, this means that your child will also say no to your pressures at times, but this process of developing one's own decision-making (i.e., autonomy) is a normal part of development. It also helps to foster self-esteem and vice-versa. Adolescents who have strong self-esteem are more likely to resist negative peer pressure. Encourage your child to develop a positive self-image by highlighting their strengths and accomplishments.

In the end, the best thing parents can do is provide guidance and support as their children navigate peer pressure. Help them develop a network of supportive friends and adults who they can turn to for help and advice. If you suspect your child is engaging in risky or harmful behavior, you should speak to your child and, if necessary, seek professional help.

What Parents Should Know about Bullying

Another area of concern in adolescent peer relationships is the impact of bullying. Bullying is a serious issue that affects many adolescents. It involves repeated and intentional aggression toward another individual with the goal of causing harm or distress. It can take many forms, including physical, verbal, and social or online bullying. Bullying can have serious negative effects on the mental health and well-being of adolescents. Victims of bullying may experience anxiety, depression, low self-esteem, and other mental health problems. Parents should be aware of the signs of bullying, including changes in their child's behavior, mood, or social interactions. Adolescents who are being bullied may become withdrawn, anxious, or avoid social situations.

Encourage your child to communicate openly and honestly with you about their experiences, and let them know that you are there to support and help them. It's also important for parents to take bullying seriously and respond appropriately. This may involve talking to the school or other authorities and seeking counseling or therapy for your child. You can also help protect your child from being bullied by promoting a culture of kindness, respect, and empathy in your home and community. Encourage your child to treat others with kindness and empathy, and to speak out against bullying when they see it happening.

Closing Advice

Positive peer relationships can have a significant impact on your child's mental health and well-being, including self-esteem, social skills, and emotional regulation. Your child is likely to seek more independence and spend more time with peers, with friendships becoming more complex and intimate. Be vigilant for signs of peer pressure and bullying. Technology and social media are changing the way adolescents form and maintain friendships, so be aware of the impact of technology on your child's peer relationships and mental health. Consider the impact of identity and cultural factors on your child's peer relationships too. You can play an important role in supporting your child's positive peer relationships by promoting communication, encouraging independence, and providing guidance and support.

> **Conversation Starters**
>
> - Can you describe a peer group that you are a part of?
> - Which activities can you participate in that might increase your acceptance into a peer group?
> - Which friends of yours do you consider a positive influence?
> - Which friends of yours do you feel like you could go to for support?
> - What type of behaviors do you feel peer pressured into?
> - What should you do if you witness someone being bullied?

Chapter 10
COMMUNICATION

How to have good conversations with your tween

Andrew C. Pool, PhD, MSc, and Eden Pontz

Adolescence is a time of tremendous potential. This phase of life, typically from about 10 through 25 years of age, offers a golden opportunity for parents and teens to connect on deep and long-lasting levels. It's also a time for parents to experience a fascinating stage in their child's development. During adolescence, children learn at a rapid pace—rivaling their first three years of life. They become super learners! Like sponges, they soak up bits of information from everywhere as they figure out who they are and want to be. They may begin to reveal sophisticated senses of humor and hold in-depth conversations about politics, societal issues, and values. Parents can start envisioning how their children will contribute to the world.

But many parents approach this time period with dread. This is because the teen years are too often painted as a time of profound storm and stress. These unfair and often flat-out-wrong messages are popularized in the media, broadcast in the news, and even conveyed in the grocery store line. Picture this: Your sweet 11-year-old lovingly rests a head on your upper arm and hugs you. The "helpful" person in line near you says, "Get those hugs in now. Soon they'll be a monster that you probably won't like." Your heart sinks and your stomach tightens. Your child senses your reaction and, worse, internalizes the message: "I am entering difficult years." But, much like you celebrate births and developmental milestones like the first words, the first steps, and the first day of school, you must appreciate adolescence and the joy it brings as your child journeys into adulthood.

Tween-ship may be making your kid far feistier and/or withdrawn than they used to be. The communication you relied on before isn't working anymore. Here are some tweaks that may help you navigate conversations.

Use Concrete Delivery

Around the age of 12 or 13, children start to identify themselves in multiple ways outside their family role. Their self-awareness among peers increases. They need to "try on different hats." As they navigate an evolving social landscape, they work to be flexible in how they present themselves. They prioritize personal values and decisions to reflect how they see themselves. Finally, they may experience greater sensitivity to feedback from others, particularly peers. It is your challenge as a parent to offer information and communicate in a way that helps your child absorb your message and own their solutions to problems.

At about 12 years old, children can better absorb information if it is delivered with a concrete mathematical structure of sorts—like "two plus two equals four." Add one, and you get five. They can better follow logic if you break the discussion down into small, concrete steps instead of a string of abstract possibilities extending into the future. You can say something like, "I understand you want to hang out with your friends on a school night. But I worry that hanging out with them might keep you from getting enough sleep. What might you do to ensure that doesn't happen?" Then let your child reflect on not getting enough sleep. When they get that, bring up the next link in the thought chain: "Do you see how not getting enough sleep might make it harder for you in school the next day? Have you ever seen that happen to your friends? How does it affect them? What are your plans to avoid that happening here?" Listen carefully to their responses and brainstorm with them. They are looking to you to be a sounding board for their ideas.

Look for signs that your tween also wants to initiate this conversation. For example, are they complaining about how tired they are at school? This is an opportunity to help them connect the dots, let them generate solutions to common problems, and learn more about who they are and who they are becoming. You can ask them why they are tired when they are at school. If they respond, "Maybe I'm not getting enough sleep at night," you might ask them whether they are staying up too late, using their phone in bed, or feeling stressed, for example. If they say, "School is so boring," consider asking them whether there is a specific class or teacher they find boring. Probe further to help them understand what may be at the root of the problem and gain further insight into their likes or dislikes.

By doing this, you acknowledge their existing wisdom and reinforce thought patterns that contribute to their safety and health. Pause at each step as they figure out things they had not considered. They are the experts in their own lives. You are their guide along their path into adulthood.

Lectures Can Backfire

It is hard for parents to watch their children make mistakes. Sometimes they're so concerned about their teens' well-being that tempers flare, and they resort to lectures. Those often lead to arguments. Cooler heads don't prevail all the time. Adults know how complicated life is and how complex relationships can be. Sometimes they can even see danger coming. You earned some of your wisdom through missteps and sometimes endured pain due to unwise choices or bad decisions. If only children could avoid making mistakes by learning from the experiences of their parents! But things don't work that way during adolescence.

You can deliver knowledge in ways that children will understand and that will help them learn to make smart decisions. However, when you tell kids what to do or warn them of dire consequences through heated and emotional lectures, you may push them away. Sometimes parents end up leading their children toward the very decisions they fear most. Consider this sample lecture:

> "Don't you know that staying up late with your friends will lead to bad grades in school? It makes me wonder what you're thinking! You might not get into a good college if you get bad grades. This wouldn't have happened if you didn't start hanging out with that group of friends. If you can't get into a good college, how will you get a good job? I'm not saying this for my own good! I know kids with bad grades who cut school. And then they start doing drugs. Do you know what happens to people who do drugs?! A lot of them die."

Does it remind you of anything you heard when you were younger?

What does the young person hear? They hear condescension and fear *but not a word you say*. Children and early adolescents think concretely, meaning they see things pretty much as they appear, at face value. It can be hard to think about the future. Instead, they live in the present as they see it.

Emotionally charged lectures also ramp up the stress level. But stressed people—especially stressed 12-year-olds—can't think abstractly. (The ability to use abstract reasoning typically happens closer to when teens start high school.) When stressed, their brain is in a state of panic, not in the "negotiating" or "thinking it through" mode. When you lecture tweens, particularly if you do so when you're panicked or upset, you heighten their fears. Tweens cannot absorb the message or use reason to understand or solve their problems in this emotional atmosphere because they can only think concretely.

How to Navigate Challenging Conversations

When your young person believes you don't think they're capable of smart behaviors, or they witness your anger but don't understand the lessons you offer, you risk moving them toward rebellion. They may set out to prove just how wrong you are. Those good intentions backfire.

But there are ways to get a lesson across to your kid. You want to honor their intelligence and encourage them to make wise decisions, so you need to change the mathematical structure of how to talk with them. It starts with adjusting it to match their stage of development. It continues with a calm delivery of the message, so you don't turn on their "panic mode" of thinking.

Let's consider the aforementioned lecture in shorthand: Your behavior now (e.g., staying up late) could lead to a dangerous outcome later, such as getting bad grades, skipping school, or using drugs, depending on a series of mysterious variables. That's algebra! It is abstract, and a 12-year-old who is panicked or not yet developmentally able to think that way won't grasp an algebra problem! But even in a panic, a person can think in concrete mathematical terms. They can understand that one plus two equals three. So, keep a few points in mind before engaging in challenging conversations:

- Choose a time and place for your discussion in which you can both remain calm.

- To successfully launch into adulthood, young people must develop their thoughts, clarify their feelings, and establish their capacity to make good decisions. Parents should aim to offer teens secure settings where they can develop their ability to be in touch with their thoughts and feelings. Doing so helps them to build a positive attitude. Ideally, these settings are bathed in calm.

- Help your teen avoid going into panic mode that will prevent them from linking actions and consequences.

How we think is tightly linked to how we feel because of the body's stress response system. Physical and emotional stress responses helped our ancestors survive. Imagine them in the jungle sensing a tiger ready to attack. They had two choices: run or fight. They chose to run, and their bodies and minds helped them survive. Blood shifted to their muscles, and their heart rate quickened to pump that blood efficiently. Their minds went into "reaction" mode rather than "problem-solving" or "feeling" mode. The mind-body connection serves a purpose—even today. Modern-day stresses have replaced the tigers, but they still activate survival mode. A key to accessing the parts of the mind that allow us to think, feel, and problem-solve is knowing how to distinguish between real tigers and paper tigers—things that might be stressful but pose no threat. Making this distinction allows for a better chance to establish calm. These points are especially true for tweens whose brains are developing rapidly. Their emotional centers are maturing at a heightened pace, making them particularly sensitive to others' reactions. This explains some of the best things about tweens, including their high energy, intense feelings, and raw empathy. It also explains some of their challenges and why they need calm settings to do their best thinking.

- Speak in a way that a concrete thinker can fully understand.

Break things down to make it easier for tweens to reach their own conclusions. See "Use Concrete Delivery" on page 104. And keep in mind that adolescents are highly sensitive to others' emotions. They feel deeply and can boldly express their feelings at times. Because you want them to think clearly, they must have the space for reflection. Sometimes they use their emotions to express their need to communicate. Let them see you role-modeling a calm state of being. When they see that, they might imitate your calmness and fold it into their ability to think, feel, and communicate.

- Be a sounding board for their suggestions.

Listen carefully when they bring up problems or complaints. These are organic, calm opportunities to have conversations about different issues. As you talk it out together, they'll feel more competent because they will have felt heard and may come up with their own solutions. They have one less reason to rebel! Before you know it, your teen may make decisions nearly as well as you do. Don't be surprised if they present a good argument, with the logic to back it up. Psychologists use the terms "hot" versus "cold" cognition—how you make decisions and think (cognition) can occur in either a "hot" (emotional or stressful) or "cold" (calm, relaxed, without emotional content) situation. Removing the emotional responses creates a better opportunity for logical problem-solving (cold cognition). You want your adolescents to develop thoughtful plans in calm settings in the hope that they will carry those decisions out even when things become challenging.

Teach Discipline in Communication

Effective communication is only one piece of the puzzle. As a parent, you want a tween who willingly tells you what's going on in their life, considers the consequences of their actions, and ultimately becomes a caring, empathetic adult. Young people talk to adults who listen. They seek adults who act as sounding boards and who will (calmly) guide them to figure things out independently. They stop talking when what they share upsets you or if you react too strongly. They do it to spare you from pain and to spare themselves from drama. When you stay calm, they keep talking. This positions you to guide them toward their better selves.

Well-disciplined young people make the wisest decisions and tend to be well-mannered and respectful. "Discipline" means to teach, not to control or punish. When your tween makes a mistake deserving of a consequence, you want them to learn. You want them to understand that consequences directly relate to their actions. On the other hand, if they feel punished or controlled, they feel like a victim and learn little. When you discipline while angry, you may pick harsher consequences that don't logically connect to what they've done. So, establish consequences in a calm, thoughtful manner.

You may not always agree with your tween's actions or choices. When you need to correct them, they must know it's because you care about them. When you get upset with them, it is essential they know it's because of how deeply you love them. If they understand how much their parent cares, they can better see the adult viewpoint. When you act out of anger, stress levels rise, and they lose the ability to understand why you feel the way you do. In their minds, you transform from the loving parent into the "tiger" readying for an attack. Anger or rage diminishes your critical influence.

However, there are times when you need to jump in—no questions asked. You didn't let your toddler put their hand on a hot stove or wander into the street. You reacted by screaming and pulling them back. And you were right to do so for their safety. There may be some "put-your-hand-on-the-stove" moments during the teen years to which you'll need to react, too. When your teen tells you they're in an unsafe situation, you respond quickly to keep your teen safe. You can focus on regaining your calm *after* they're safe. Consider using a Code Word (see page 130) to help them escape a dangerous situation.

You are a role model 24/7. If you make it look like nothing flusters you, you're missing an opportunity to guide your adolescent in managing stress. And you'll probably be faking it. It's okay to say aloud, "Right now, I'm so upset that I can't make decisions or give consequences. I want to think this through instead of just reacting. I love you. For both of us, I'm going to calm myself down. We'll talk when we're both ready." Then, take care of yourself. Do what you need to do to process your thoughts and feelings. Come back when you're ready to support your tween to learn to do the same.

Closing Advice

Knowing it is vital to be calm when communicating with your 12-year-old doesn't make it easy—not by a long shot. But a mindful combination of listening, modeling calmness, brainstorming solutions, and allowing tweens to own those solutions positions you to guide your child toward adulthood with love.

Many of the ideas in this chapter are informed by Dr. Ken Ginsburg and our work at the Center for Parent and Teen Communication.

Conversation Starters

- What are some of the traits that you think make you different from others in the family? What do you admire about your siblings? How do you think you're different from your siblings? How can I help you become your best self?

- Who are some of your friends now that make you feel good when you spend time with them? Do you wish you could change anything about your group of friends? Who could you be nicer to?

- What are some important qualities that people can have? What values do you see in your friends that you disagree with?

- What are some things you think you're good at? Do you show these things to others? What do you do if you find that you're not so good at something—how do you make up for that?

- What strong beliefs do you have right now? Do you have a particular belief that you wish you could learn more about?

Chapter 11
RESILIENCE

How to help your tweens learn to help themselves

Lacey Rosenbaum, PhD, MEd

Have you ever looked back on a difficult time in your life, maybe the early years of parenting, the COVID-19 pandemic, or the loss of a loved one, and wondered how you survived that? When we face a difficult situation and get through it, and maybe even learn and grow from the experience, we call this **resilience.**

I am a psychologist and researcher who studies resilience in young people. I work with educators, parents, and caregivers to teach them how to help kids become more resilient and emotionally healthy. I am also the mother of two children. Based on my research, professional work, and parenting experience, I know that helping our children develop resilience is one of the most meaningful gifts we can give them.

At 12, your tween's life is becoming more complicated, and their self-esteem is taking a beating. While our temptation may be to step in and make their hurts go away—as we used to do when they were little—the far more effective and long-term solution is to turn our attention toward resilience-building. When we help kids build resilience, we help them learn to help themselves. We all want to raise kids who can face life's adversities, struggle well, and bounce back.

This chapter addresses common questions that I get asked by students, parents, and teachers about resilience. I also include research-based strategies translated into practical things that you can start doing with your child immediately. While there is no perfect formula or script, I have included some sample language to get you started.

Commonly Asked Questions about Resilience

The best news I can share is that a supportive and stable relationship with a caregiver is the number one predictor that children will develop resilience. Given that you are reading this book and this chapter, you are well on your way to raising a resilient human.

What Is Resilience?

Resilience is an individual's ability to bounce back from challenging experiences or adapt when faced with hard times. Resilience refers to both the process of struggling well and the outcome of successfully getting through difficult life experiences, according to the American Psychological Association. Resilience doesn't mean figuring it out all on your own. In fact, being able to reach out to others for support is a crucial part of resilience. For kids, it's up to families, communities, and government to provide help and support.

Are Kids Born Resilient or Can It Be Learned?

Resilience is not something kids are born with. Resilience can be learned, practiced, and developed as kids grow. It's an important character trait because everyone faces daily challenges and setbacks throughout life. The more opportunities kids have to develop their resiliency muscles, the more likely they will be able to sit with future struggles and move through their challenges. For our kids to be resilient in the face of adversity, they need love, safety, security, and connection so they have a strong system of support to help them navigate the challenges.

I like to use trees as an analogy for how resilience develops in kids. To withstand the resistance of a strong wind or storm, a tree needs a wide network of roots that reach deep into the ground to prevent it from being toppled over. Kids need these roots of support from parents and other adults to help them withstand a tough time. And a tree does something else in response to repeated environmental stress. It grows something called "reaction wood" to give itself extra strength to stay upright and adapt well. Our kids do this too. They grow their resiliency muscles when faced with repeated challenges. These resilience muscles help them stay upright, adapt, and develop into healthy adults.

What about Children and Families Who Experience Serious Hardship?

Many young people and their families face serious challenges like divorce, loss of loved ones, financial insecurity, systematic oppression, violence, or other trauma. And some kids have challenges because of disability, learning difficulties or disorders, mental health challenges, and chronic health conditions. While individual resilience can help with all these challenges, children and families should not be burdened with managing these difficulties alone. Children are more likely to adapt to adversity and threats when their basic human needs are nurtured and supported. Government, schools, and communities play an important role in providing safe places for children and their families to live, learn, play, and grow.

Resilience won't make problems go away. Still, resilience can help kids get more enjoyment in life and better handle stress. Research also shows that resilience can help protect kids from various mental health challenges, such as depression and anxiety.

Why Is Resilience Important for 12-Year-Olds?

All young people face everyday challenges, like arguments with friends, disappointing test results, or sporting losses. Your child needs resilience to bounce back and learn from these challenges. Twelve-year-olds are figuring out who they are as they move from child to young adult. They are sorting out their unique place in their family, school, and community. They are coming to terms with their changing bodies, gender and sexuality, race, culture, religion, ability level in various activities, and more. Plus, they are navigating the influence of technology, social media, constant access to information, and peer pressure. Research suggests that there are higher rates of stress and mental health challenges like depression and anxiety being experienced by middle school students compared to a decade ago. Teaching our kids to cope with life and become resilient is critical to their ability to overcome stress and help with anxiety and depression.

> ### For More Help
>
> Developing resilience looks different in each child. If your child is stuck or overwhelmed and unable to cope, you may want to consider having them talk to someone who can help, such as a school counselor, psychologist, other mental health professional, or their pediatrician or primary care doctor.

What Can Parents Do to Help Their Children Become Resilient?

The most influential protective factor is at least one stable and committed relationship with a supportive parent, caregiver, or another adult. And the more positive adults in a child's life, the more likely they are to become resilient. Experts agree that some parenting practices can make a difference, no matter your family context or the challenges your child might face. Researchers have identified specific qualities that help kids develop resilience:

- Recognizing and expressing their emotions.
- Using healthy coping strategies to help manage stress.
- Problem-solving skills.
- Having a growth mindset, the belief that if you keep trying, you can learn to do new things, even if you make mistakes or aren't successful the first few times.

There are also important external supports that help kids develop resilience, just like tree roots. These include access to:

- Positive adults
- Schools
- Extracurricular activities such as sports, music, drama, or social justice clubs
- Community programs, including mentoring
- Parks and community spaces
- Religious institutions
- Cultural groups
- Health and mental health systems

Resilience won't happen in one day or with one conversation. It happens over time as kids see resilience modeled by their parents and caregivers and as they are supported to face challenges, make mistakes, and learn from their experiences. Teaching your child that it is okay to ask for help and that you don't have to "tough out" challenges alone is a vital message.

The list below gives three practices to help build resilience in your child.

1. Model Resilience Yourself

You have the most influence over your child's attitudes and behaviors. It is important to model being resilient yourself. You don't have to be perfect. We all make mistakes, and we all face tough times.

- Show your vulnerability. You can demonstrate coping skills, including apologizing, forgiving, and bouncing back from a challenge.
- Share what you learned or will do differently next time with your child.
- Care for yourself mentally and physically, set boundaries, and seek help when needed.

Modeling these positive behaviors helps teach your child that mistakes aren't the end of the world and can be an opportunity to grow and improve. Using humor in the face of mistakes or difficulties is another positive tool you can model for your child. Consider how you want your child to handle life challenges and lead by example. This might sound like this:

> "Wow, I had such a rough day. My boss didn't like the project I turned in, and I felt so embarrassed during our team meeting when she said it was not my best effort. I am a little distracted

right now. Please give me a few minutes to catch my breath and write down a few ideas about how I will respond to my boss tomorrow. Then I really want to make some dinner together and watch our favorite show. Spending time with you always makes me feel better."

2. Empathize When Your Child Struggles

Not only is your kid looking at how you handle difficult situations, but they are also looking at how you handle the situation when *they* face a challenge. Consider a moment where your child comes home from school and is visibly upset because they didn't make the sports team, got a low grade, or were not invited to a peer's party. If you are uncomfortable with your child's emotions and are quick to dismiss them as silly "kid" worries, or if you ask them to forget about it and move on, it sends a message that those feelings are inconvenient, not okay, and best buried or avoided, as something to feel guilt or shame about.

- Create a safe space for your child to share with you anything they are experiencing.
- Remove distractions and really listen without judgment.
- Put yourself in your child's shoes and imagine how they must feel. Our kids need us to be okay with their complicated feelings, as painful as it can be to see them struggle.

Your child might be experiencing rejection, anger, sadness, anxiety, or disappointment. When you respond, remember that you don't have to take away their pain (as much as you wish you could) or have the perfect thing to say. You simply need to assure them that you are there for them no matter what. If they don't want to talk, let them know you will be there to listen when they are ready. This might sound like this:

"I am sorry that you weren't invited to the party. Thanks for telling me. It can be really hurtful when we aren't included. I am here for you. Is there anything I can do right now that might make you feel better?"

3. Let Your Child Make Mistakes

It can be difficult to watch your child make mistakes or not do their best at school or home. We often want to fix the situation when they face a setback. As hard as it is to let your child make mistakes, it must happen for them to develop resiliency. If your child never makes mistakes, they'll never learn how to process complicated feelings and make different choices next time. Experiencing failure can help children learn coping skills, perseverance, and problem-solving.

- Assure your child that it is normal to feel upset when things don't go the way we want them. Remind your child that the painful feelings won't last forever.
- Practice curiosity and avoid viewing experiences as good/bad or success/failure.

Kids need to hear parents say it is okay to make mistakes, to not get the perfect grade, or to not make the sports team. Encouraging your child to embrace a growth mindset will help them become resilient, persistent, and eager to tackle challenges head-on. This might sound like this:

"Thanks for telling me about your math test. It is so hard when we don't get the grade we want. I am not worried about this grade if you feel you did your best. When you feel up for it, I would be glad to help you brainstorm ways to prepare for the next math test."

Closing Advice

Learning how to cope with adversity is integral to healthy adolescent development. Our kids demonstrate resilience in the face of challenges by reaching out to systems of support and building their resilience muscles with practice. A supportive and stable relationship with a caregiver is the number one predictor that children will develop resilience. You can model resilience, empathize when your child struggles, and let your child make mistakes. Mistakes help us overcome difficult times, learn from the experience, and keep trying.

Chapter 12
RISK-TAKING

How to encourage your tween to make safe choices

Andrew C. Pool, Phd, MSc, and Eden Pontz

Young people spend much of adolescence preparing themselves to move into adulthood. As part of those preparations, they must explore new opportunities and take risks. It's by doing so that they gain the necessary practice to make the big jump into adulthood later. The parent's role is to help ensure this practice is useful and encourage them to make safe choices.

There are at least three daunting leaps a 12-year-old is starting to think about:

1. **Leaving home.** Until now, your 12-year-old has assumed you will take care of what's needed. After all, you have provided shelter, food, and entertainment for the last 11 years! Thinking about leaving a comfortable home where most of your needs are met seems almost...unthinkable. But it's around now that

your child begins to imagine a time in which they can care for themselves. They may begin reasoning, "I am not my parents or siblings. I am my own person. Someday I'll make a home of my own. I need to show my parent(s) that I don't need them to meet my needs like they did in the past."

2. **Finding their life's work.** People have asked, "What do you want to do when you grow up?" since your child was little. And while they may have been sure what they wanted to do when they were four or five years old, the answer is no longer so obvious or easy by the age of 12. Twelve-year-olds must begin to imagine how they will contribute to the world, support themselves (and maybe others), and pay the bills. There is a wide array of choices. One way to discover where they fit in is to eliminate places they don't. To do that, your young person needs to try out many different roles outside their home. They may ask themselves, "Why don't I know what I want to do when I grow up? Am I supposed to know by now or by the time I graduate high school? Maybe I'll know by the time I apply to college? I better get out there now and start figuring out what I'm good at."

3. **Finding a life partner.** It's hard to believe that your 12-year-old may be thinking about romance. After all, you might have just seen them drawing a comic book or learning magic tricks or playing in the dirt with friends and having a great time! But they may be starting to think about the types of people they are attracted to and what kinds of qualities they'd want in a long-term partner. From puppy love to a first crush, your tween may experience feelings that provide an opportunity to start learning about healthy relationships. One of the ways they'll improve their chance of finding that special someone is by meeting new people and having different relationships first. This may be the first time they think, "I hope I find someone who finds me attractive."

Taking chances and, yes, maybe failing, is necessary during adolescence. Tweens and teens can learn as much about themselves through their failures as they can from their successes. Parents play two critical roles during this time of great opportunity: supporting their kids' healthy risk-taking and protecting them from unhealthy risks.

Support Healthy Risk-Taking

The ways in which 12-year-olds test limits can seem limitless! You might be surprised to hear them ask to walk to school or take public transportation by themselves. Perhaps they ask to stay out late with friends on a school night. Or they express an interest in watching movies or shows with adult themes. You can use scenarios like these to create safe growth opportunities. For example, you can surround your child with adults who act as positive influences, such as mentors, coaches, or family friends. Steer your tween toward new opportunities within the community, like a part-time job babysitting or walking a neighbor's dog. Help them find new ways to broaden their social circles by doing an activity they enjoy. Here are five ways to support your tween's healthy development.

1. **Help them find their inner athlete.** Participation in sports allows young people to learn to try, fail, and recover. They may learn accountability, dedication, and how to receive and implement feedback. Sports also teach the importance of collaboration, camaraderie, and leadership. Even if they discover they aren't athletic, they can still get involved in the different aspects of helping to manage a team.

2. **Get them to join in.** Joining organized clubs and after-school activities lets young people check out new areas that pique their interest. These groups offer the chance to develop skills they don't learn in school. They also allow your child to meet up with others who may share a common interest.

3. **Suggest they try out.** Trying out for plays, contests, debates, and competitions permits tweens and teens to test themselves safely. When they occasionally fail, they may learn to try something different next time. They can also learn what healthy competition entails and the traits of good sportsmanship.

4. **Show them the importance of work done well.** Few think of cleaning, doing chores, or paying bills as "risky." Yet learning, managing, and finishing tasks is essential practice for when they will be holding down their own fort. These important opportunities teach tweens responsibility, build a work ethic, and help them to build self-reliance and life skills.

5. **Encourage them to build a social life.** Having an active social life that includes friends, peers, and romantic interests are important aspects of adolescence. Your tween will learn that building and maintaining relationships can be challenging at times and they may experience both joy and heartbreak. But tweens must have the chance to practice relationships to prepare them for the ups and downs they'll encounter in the workplace and in adult relationships.

Much of adolescence is spent determining where you fit in and discovering your identity in relation to those around you—family, peers, or others in your community. Along the way, you work to find out what makes you unique. That includes figuring out the strengths that will allow you to contribute to your community and your limitations and how to work around them. You must spend time learning how to manage challenges effectively and bounce back from failure. And you need time to figure out your values and beliefs and how they may differ from your family's or society's. Now is the time that your 12-year-old will start envisioning what it's like to be independent.

There's no replacement for the caring adults who get involved in helping tweens figure out who they are and who they want to be. But it can be hard for adults to know when to stand back, when to jump in, when to let tweens try, and when to let them fail. What's the best way to pass along the lessons of personal insight and wisdom gained through firsthand experience?

One place to start is by assuring your teen that the hard questions they keep asking themselves as they work to form their identity can take years to answer. Remind them, too, that none of their answers are set in stone. The choices they make may change as they move forward. Life offers many chances to reconsider one's place in family and community and to remake yourself if things didn't work well the first time. Adolescence involves a lot of trial and error to determine likes and dislikes as well as strengths and weaknesses. For example, your child may have been the star of their youth baseball team, but when they reached middle school, they faced much greater competition and realized they don't like playing baseball as much as they once did. However, the school play grabbed their attention. They took the risk and tried out, and this opened them up to new peers and experiences.

It's not always easy to be a responsible parent. Part of being responsible requires you to be flexible at times. However, when it comes to safety issues or serious challenges to values or morals, those are the times to establish firm, clear, and consistent boundaries. Safety and morality issues can arise when it comes to things like drugs, alcohol, unsafe driving, or sex. Even if your tween complains that you're being too strict, know that 12-year-olds need firm boundaries to ensure security. They *want* to feel safe. When you give them clear boundaries backed by safety, you offer them the "edges" they can push against but not go beyond.

Protect Against Unhealthy Risks

Parents and caregivers must be firm and hold their tweens and teens to high expectations. If their behavior threatens safety, they must hear your voice saying, "Don't do it." If a situation compromises morality, parents must draw the line. Your 12-year-old will thrive when adults establish clear expectations about behaviors that are not allowed.

The challenge? While we want to protect children as they grow, there is such a thing as overprotection. Children need chances to make their way through different real-life challenges. By doing so, they learn to succeed and fail. If they don't get these chances, they may come to believe that their parents don't have confidence in them. So, throughout adolescence, parents must find a balance that allows tweens to test boundaries while remaining safe. Think about a time when your child was younger. It was fine for your child to spill flour on the floor as you showed them how to make chocolate chip cookies. You didn't mind if they accidentally splattered eggs on the counter when they mixed ingredients. But it was never okay for them to put their hands on the hot oven rack or to retrieve finished cookie pans without using a potholder. Now that they are 12 years old, ask yourself, what are the "hot oven" issues they face today?

To ensure your child meets your expectations, you must begin communicating with your 12-year-old in three key areas. Make clear and firm statements about:

- Substance use: drugs and alcohol
- How to protect your body and respect others' bodies: safeguarding yourself physically and emotionally in romantic or sexual situations
- Riding in a car: wearing a seatbelt, avoiding distractions, and understanding potentially dangerous situations (drugs/alcohol combined with driving), and what to do if the police stop the car

This list is not complete, as your family may have other important issues to add. These, too, deserve conversations in which you set clear expectations. When you establish these expectations, consider your child's individual development to ensure they will clearly understand.

Set Boundaries

You likely remember the thrills that came with pushing boundaries set for you by your parents. Part of the reason it was a thrill is because you were doing what tweens are supposed to do—test limits and expand boundaries. The teen years are the time to establish new forms of freedom and limits. But 12-year-olds need parents to set boundaries and controls at a pace that matches their development and maturity. This isn't about parents controlling anything or anyone. Instead, it's about giving tweens the gift of *self-control*.

Before establishing limits with your 12-year-old, start the conversation with something positive. Let them know you love them. Remind them how important they are and what their well-being means to you. Give them an example of something they've done that makes you proud. As you turn the conversation toward setting boundaries, be sure they understand the point is to keep them safe, not to control them or ruin a good time. Tell them you're on their side. As you talk about boundaries together, they'll be more likely to listen and respect what you establish.

Don't wait until the teen years to set boundaries. By establishing them consistently when children are younger (e.g., "Don't cross the street without stopping and holding my hand"), your 12-year-old will understand what's expected. Then, when you set new limits (e.g., "Yes, you can ride your bike to your friend's house but wear your helmet"), you're reinforcing what you've already been doing for a while. As they get older and prove themselves trustworthy by showing responsibility and making wise choices, you'll be able to reassess and be more flexible about specific boundaries.

Think about the time and place when establishing boundaries. Choose a time when you and your teen are calm. If you try to establish boundaries when either of you are angry or upset, your teen may think the boundaries are connected to punishment. Choose a time of day when your teen is awake, alert, and relaxed. Let them know in advance what you'll be talking about, if possible. Choose a place where you both feel comfortable, safe, and calm, such as your living room or a walk together around your neighborhood.

It's okay to ask your child what they think is reasonable as you create boundaries. Explain that you are willing to negotiate—to a point. Know if you are too strict, they may rebel against your rules. But make it clear that you'll stand firm when safety or morality is at risk. Tell them you're willing to revisit rules after a while—*if* they've earned your trust by proving that they can adhere to limits you've set.

When parents lead by example, they show tweens it's possible to live within various boundaries set in their lives. So, even though it's hard to drive the speed limit when you're in a rush, it's set for your safety and that of others, so you do it. If you know you'll come home later than expected, you should let your family know where you are. When parents show how to live within reasonable limits, tweens are more likely to accept the boundaries set for them.

Try to allow for natural consequences to be felt when limits are pushed too far. If your child insists on staying out late with friends on a school night and is exhausted and struggling in school the next day, they may learn the lesson that they need more sleep at night. If you have set a particular consequence for your child, follow through when they break rules. It's essential to maintain your credibility and reinforce that boundaries are important. Don't establish consequences that you are unable to follow through on.

Use a Code Word

Code words give young people a way to signal to their parents that they want to get out of an uncomfortable or even dangerous situation without their peers knowing. If you've never used a code word, work with your tween to get started. Choose a code word (or phrase) that your preteen can remember and use if they find themselves in a tight spot. They must never share the word with their friends, or it becomes useless. Just as "1234" or birthdays are not secure codes for bank accounts, be thoughtful about choosing words that are secure, memorable, and 12-year-old user-friendly. Poor choices for code words include nonsensical or obvious words, such as "Timeout123#@!", "HELP!!!", or "Coconut." Choose a word that can be easily worked into a sentence, text, or phone call in a way that will be noticeable to a parent but not obvious to other tweens or teens.

Here are some examples of better choices:

- Dad, I think I left the **door unlocked.**
- Sorry! Mom, you said **Aunt Julie** was coming over tonight, but I'm with friends. Can I see her tomorrow?
- I won't be back in time to walk **Spotty.** Can you take him out?

Here's how it works:

1. Your tween tells friends that they have to call or text home. They can complain the entire time. "My parents are so frustrating. They make me check in with them. If I don't, they freak out."

2. Your tween calls or texts in front of friends so they can hear or see the conversation.

3. You notice the code word or phrase and contact your tween. You say they need to come home.

4. If it is easy for your tween to get home, they leave, while complaining about their "totally unreasonable parents."

5. If your tween can't get home on their own, they argue out loud. "What do you mean I have to come home? You're being so unfair!"

6. That's your cue that your tween has no easy way home, and you elevate the suggestion to a demand. "Where are you?! Be outside in a few minutes. I'm coming to pick you up!"

7. You arrive and tell your tween (out of earshot of peers) how proud you are that they asked for help. "I'm proud of you for using our code word. I'm happy you're safe. I can take your friends home, too, if they want to leave."

Using a code word and taking the blame as the parent allows your 12-year-old to save face. When they do the right thing, praise them for making a level-headed decision. That's not the time to punish them for being in a challenging situation in the first place. If you punish your 12-year-old, you can be pretty sure they will never use this strategy again. Be grateful they have mastered this skill and stayed safe. Depending on your word choice, you may want to create a new one, so the code is not cracked.

Many of the ideas in this chapter are informed by Dr. Ken Ginsburg and our work at the Center for Parent and Teen Communication.

Conversation Starters

- What's an accomplishment you're proud of? How did you accomplish it, and how could you use those skills down the line?
- What are some attributes you think make a person successful?
- What worries you most about the future: attending high school or college or getting a job?
- What is something you like to do when you're bored?
- What talents or skills have you discovered you have?
- If you could be doing anything outside of school right now, what would it be and why? Given a chance, would you like to incorporate that into a job? Why or why not?
- What do you dream of doing when you get older? Can you do anything now to help you accomplish that goal?
- What topic could you talk about for hours?
- What are some things that give your life meaning and purpose?
- What do you think makes a good friend? Do you have more good friends inside or outside of school?
- Is there anyone at school you'd like to get to know better? Why?
- Are there people in romantic relationships at your school?
- What's your favorite show or performer these days?
- When do you know you can trust someone?
- What traits do you look for when trying to make a new friend?
- What do you think are some key things to keep in mind when it comes to dating someone?

Chapter 13
NAVIGATING THE ADHD MAZE

How to support your child and yourself

Jennifer Gentile, PsyD
Staff Psychologist, Boston Children's Hospital
& Harvard Medical School; Chief Clinical Officer
THYNK, Inc.

The preteen years are full of battles over everything from homework to chores. An adolescent's emotions can go from high to low in a matter of minutes. The struggle for independence is real—and it's perfectly ordinary. But for kids who have been diagnosed with attention deficit/hyperactivity disorder (ADHD)—and that's 13% of all 12-year-olds—the highs can be higher, the lows can be lower, and all those ordinary battles can be extraordinarily intense. The good news for kids (and their parents!) is that the medical community understands ADHD far more than it did just five years ago and has better ways to diagnose and treat ADHD, ranging from coaching and therapy to medication and technological interventions.

ADHD Decoded

So, what exactly is ADHD? Attention-deficit/hyperactivity disorder is a neurodevelopmental condition that affects a person's ability to focus, control impulses, and regulate their energy levels and emotions. But it's more than just "being hyper" or "having a short attention span." In fact, doctors often describe ADHD as a disorder of executive functioning skills— which include attention, concentration, impulse control, decision-making, prioritization, and planning. ADHD comes in three subtypes: "primarily inattentive," "primarily hyperactive-impulsive," and "combined presentation." Understanding which type of ADHD your child has, and what to expect from each type, ensures that you can offer them tailored support.

If you hear "ADHD" and conjure images of little kids bouncing off the walls, you'll need to set those aside. ADHD manifests much differently in preteens. Twelve-year-olds with ADHD often struggle with organizing tasks, completing homework, and staying focused during class. They might lose things or not pay attention to details or tasks that don't interest them. Some kids may lie impulsively and, when asked why they lie, they don't have a good answer other than they didn't think before they spoke. Just as kids with ADHD may behave impulsively, they may speak impulsively as well.

By age 12, there are gender-specific differences, too.

Boys:

- Hyperactivity is often more evident in boys with ADHD. They may fidget, squirm, and struggle to sit still.
- Impulsivity tends to be more common. Boys may act before thinking, leading to impulsive decisions and sometimes risky behaviors.

- Boys with ADHD might be more prone to physical aggression and confrontations with peers.
- Academic struggles are common, especially in subjects that require sustained attention and organization.

Girls:

- Girls with ADHD tend to be less hyperactive and impulsive. They may appear quieter and less disruptive in the classroom but tend to daydream more than boys.
- Girls tend to internalize their struggles, leading to anxiety and low self-esteem. They may become perfectionists, fearing mistakes and criticism.
- Social difficulties are common, as girls with ADHD may struggle with maintaining friendships and navigating social nuances.
- Many girls with ADHD are overlooked or misdiagnosed because their symptoms are less noticeable or less disruptive than boys' symptoms.
- ADHD is affected by mood, and menstrual cycles can multiply symptoms.

Diagnostic Challenges

Properly diagnosing ADHD generally involves interviews and standardized assessments. If you or your child suspects ADHD, start by setting up a visit with your child's pediatrician or doctor to explain what kinds of symptoms brought you in. Your doctor will probably ask you and your child some questions and provide several forms to be filled out by family members and teachers, asking them to report any atypical behavior they may have noticed. The doctor may also suggest that your child see a therapist or refer your child to a neuropsychologist for more testing. Depending on the doctor's confidence in the diagnosis, they may prescribe medication or refer you to a child psychiatrist for that.

Once a diagnosis is confirmed, it can be helpful to share the diagnosis with your child's school, as there may be accommodations that can be put in place to improve your child's academic success. A common accommodation for a child with ADHD is a 504 plan, which is designed to remove any barriers limiting a child's ability to receive an appropriate education. A 504 plan for a child with ADHD may involve seating the child at the front of the class, allowing extra time to complete work, breaking long assignments into smaller chunks, and pairing written instructions with oral instructions.

ADHD is commonly underdiagnosed and misdiagnosed. That's because, in approximately 70% of children, the disorder coexists with other diagnoses, such as depression, anxiety, learning disabilities, or autism. It's also because disruptive behaviors are often misinterpreted as aggression, inattention is misinterpreted as ignoring, and lack of focus is misinterpreted as laziness or carelessness. Indeed, the symptoms of ADHD often are initially perceived as willful and/or character-driven, and children may not be given the benefit of the doubt when they are actually trying to make good and appropriate decisions.

ADHD Intervention

Stimulant medications are usually the first-choice treatment for ADHD. These come in several varieties and classes, but probably the most important distinction is long-acting versus short-acting. Short-acting medications may produce results in the morning but wear off after lunch. Long-acting medications may work for longer but keep your child up at night or suppress their appetite. Medications do not work for all children and medications are not without side effects.

If your child's provider recommends medication, it will usually be in conjunction with a non-medication intervention such as the ones discussed below. A thorough review of pharmaceutical options is best left to your child's doctor.

Outpatient therapy can help your child gain insight and establish strategies and tools to manage their symptoms, particularly if they suffer from anxiety or depression. It's important to note that poorly treated depression or anxiety can make ADHD symptoms worse.

Coaches, more specifically executive function coaches, can help with strategies to improve organization, structure time, prioritize goals, and develop systems that provide external executive function for your child, such as phone reminders to help memory, behavior supports to encourage good decision making, and visual prompts/aids to help with prioritization, decision making, planning, and calendering.

Family therapy not only helps the child with ADHD, but it also helps the family system and individual family members. In family therapy, caregivers learn how to create a home environment where the child can excel. Jointly developed behavioral systems cultivated in therapy work to reinforce desired behaviors and decrease challenging behaviors in the home. Family therapy also provides a safe environment to discuss family members' experiences and feelings.

Digital organization is what it sounds like: using a phone, laptop, or other electronic device to keep organized and "off-load" information—that is, free up space in your brain by recording information and setting automatic reminders. Calendars, day planners, email, timers, and notepad apps all help with off-loading. These same devices can act as memory triggers, particularly when the child could use some extra time to transition from one activity to another. This is all best done with some automation—"set it and forget it"—but will surely need a manual touch from time to time.

Digital interventions are electronic tools designed specifically to improve symptoms of ADHD. Some are video games that improve symptoms when the games are played multiple times a week during several weeks. There is even a video game that uses an EEG headset (a wearable device for electroencephalography, a monitoring method to record the electrical activity of the brain) to measure when the child is paying attention. With this game, when the child is paying attention, the character moves in the game, which teaches the player how and when to pay attention, how to improve impulse control, and how to make more thoughtful decisions. Video games are also available that have been shown to decrease frustration and improve the management of anger and angry outbursts. Cognitive therapy apps targeting the symptoms and challenges of ADHD may help a child develop new skills and reinforce improvements over time.

If you are considering using a digital intervention, make sure that the tool uses evidence-based techniques. And if you end up using several of these digital options or none, don't forget to limit your preteen's total screen time, especially around bedtime.

Finally, a word of caution about social media. Medical literature is full of articles on the negative effect social media has on preteens. Preteens and teens who engage more on social media are at higher risk of anxiety and depression, which compounds the effects from ADHD. If your child is on social media at all, remember to review what they are watching and posting.

Putting It Together: Meet Jamie, a 12-Year-Old with ADHD

Jamie, a bright and imaginative 12-year-old, has always been a whirlwind of energy. She's the kind of child who can't sit still for long, is always on the move, and is described as a "chatterbox" by teachers. Her parents, Alex and Madison, had noticed her boundless energy from a young age but chalked it up to having an active child. As this was their first child, they didn't have anyone to compare her to.

As Jamie entered sixth grade, her behavior and school performance began to raise concerns. She struggled to finish her homework or forgot to hand it in. Her room was a mess, with clothes and sports equipment scattered everywhere. In school, while she excelled in subjects she was passionate about—like art and science—her grades in subjects she found more "boring," such as math and English, were inconsistent.

By the end of sixth grade, Jamie also had trouble making and keeping friends. She often interrupted others in conversations and was unaware of personal boundaries. Her boundless energy, deemed "cute" in early elementary school, morphed into her being called "annoying" by peers in middle school.

Alex and Madison consulted their pediatrician, who referred them to a child psychologist for a comprehensive evaluation. After a series of assessments and interviews, Jamie received a diagnosis of attention-deficit/hyperactivity disorder, primarily inattentive presentation. Jamie began taking a low dose of the drug Ritalin and started working with an executive function coach. With her permission, Jamie's parents spoke with her school guidance counselor and Jamie was put on a 504 plan at school.

How to Support Your Kid—and Yourself

How can you support your 12-year-old with ADHD? Here are some strategies to consider:

1. **Structure routines.** Establish clear daily routines to help your child stay on track. Some kids may need a list in the morning like "clothes, breakfast, teeth, backpack, water bottle." Setting alarms or routines on devices helps.

2. **Break tasks into small steps.** Break down tasks into manageable chunks to prevent overwhelm. For example, instead of "clean your room," say, "put the dirty clothes in the hamper and the clean clothes in your closet." Then, check in often.

3. **Communicate openly.** Encourage your child to talk about their struggles and feelings without judgment. Because your 12-year-old is soon entering teenagerdom, a talk therapist can come in handy.

4. **Use visual aids.** Visual schedules and charts can aid in task completion and organization. Smartphone calendars are excellent for people with ADHD.

5. **Beware of boredom.** People with ADHD may not be as intrinsically motivated to do non-preferred tasks. Setting a time limit for a boring task can help.

6. **Try behavioral therapy.** Explore therapy options such as cognitive behavioral therapy (CBT). Talk therapy can help promote effective coping, improve uptake of strategies, and help catch other mental health conditions early.

7. **Download some apps.** Several apps are available that seek to improve attention through games, which challenge different parts of a person's attention. Just beware of digital overuse.

8. **Be patient.** People with ADHD can seem forgetful, like they're not paying attention (they aren't, but they may be trying to!), or inconsiderate. Get curious, not furious! Ask questions such as, "Can you repeat what I just told you?" rather than being punitive.

9. **Celebrate progress.** Focus on the positives and celebrate your child's achievements. People with ADHD get a lot of negative feedback from the world. "Where's your homework?", "You're on the wrong bus", or "You forgot to meet me." So, try to build them up. Celebrate preparation and effort, not just outcomes.

10. **Advocate for your child.** Work closely with teachers and school staff to create an accommodating environment. Small changes in school can reap huge rewards. Some kids may need a 504 plan or even an Individualized Education Program (IEP) for the right accommodations.

11. **Take care of yourself.** Children with ADHD are wonderful and amazing AND they often require an abundance of patience and persistence. Please take care of yourself. Get some rest. And don't go it alone: Engage teachers, doctors, and therapists, and take advantage of modern technology.

12. **Be ready to pivot.** Teenagers grow fast. They may need their medications adjusted, and new roles (e.g., babysitting or joining a team) may require new strategies and reminders.

Closing Advice

We are all unique in the way we think, act, and learn. ADHD may present challenges, but it also brings strengths like creativity, energy, flexibility in thinking, and resilience. Your role is to help your 12-year-old harness these strengths and navigate the twists and turns of their different but remarkable journey.

Conversation Starters

- I noticed you've been having a hard time staying organized with your schoolwork. How can we help you create a routine that works for you?

- Do you ever feel like your mind is going a million miles an hour? Let's talk about strategies to manage that.

- What are some things that make it easier for you to concentrate? Let's try to incorporate those into your study time.

- Remember when we talked about setting goals? How's that going for you? Any progress you're proud of?

- If there was one thing you'd like me to understand better about your ADHD, what would it be?

- What are some fun activities or hobbies you enjoy that help you unwind and relax?

Chapter 14
MANAGING CHRONIC ILLNESS

How you can support the transition to adolescence

Sarah Jaser, PhD

Parenting a child with a chronic health condition is not easy, and responsibility for daily management transitions from parents to their children during adolescence, adding a new layer of complexity. It's common for both kids and their parents to experience burnout, frustration, or lack of motivation for care, and it can be tempting for parents to back off and let kids take over control of their health care. But research supports the fact that ongoing parental involvement is one of the strongest predictors of better outcomes—for both physical health and quality of life. Adolescence is also a time of incredible growth and change, and for some kids with chronic health conditions, this is a time when they find joy in connecting with other kids facing similar challenges or they take on new roles in advocacy and outreach.

As a licensed clinical psychologist who has been conducting research and working with children and adolescents with diabetes and their families for more than 15 years, my expertise is in pediatric diabetes, but many of these recommendations apply to other chronic health conditions as well.

Parental Monitoring

Parental monitoring involves regular contact with adolescents regarding their daily activities, as well as knowledge about and supervision of those activities. Monitoring your child is an important part of parenting during adolescence, but this does not mean simply "tracking" your child's movements. Monitoring can be both direct, like checking to see if your child has absences or missing assignments on a school website, or indirect, such as asking about how classes are going. Monitoring can include things like asking your child about their friends—who they sit with at lunch, who is in their group for a class project, who else is going to a sleepover or meeting them at the mall. This could also look like reviewing social media together— sitting together and checking out their friends' Instagram stories or Snap Stories or asking them about their best friends/close friends lists. By approaching this in a collaborative way rather than a punitive one, kids are more likely to share information. And by asking questions and learning about a child's life on a regular basis, a parent will have more context for situations that may arise. For example, they might know if a person who got in trouble at school is someone whom their child has known for years and is trying to maintain a friendship with or is a newcomer whose behavior may warrant a more serious conversation.

For parents of kids with chronic health conditions, monitoring can take on a different meaning. Many kids with diabetes use continuous glucose monitors, which provide ongoing data about glucose levels, and this data can be shared with parents or other adults, like the school nurse. This type of information shows a parent how the child is doing with diabetes management, but without context, it can be easy to jump to conclusions, like, "you must have eaten something sweet if your blood sugar is this high." It is also common (and understandable) for parents of kids with chronic health conditions to frequently ask their child about symptoms. Some of this checking in is helpful and necessary, but it can also become aversive to kids if they feel that is the first, or only, thing their parents want to know about.

Like other forms of structure, monitoring works best when it is in the context of warm and supportive parenting. If kids feel that all parents care about is where they are, who they're with, or how they're taking care of their illness (e.g., taking medications, following treatment regimen), it becomes intrusive. But if monitoring is just one part of their interaction, which also includes non-judgmental listening, humor, and fun activities, it will feel more supportive.

Collaborative Management

For children with chronic health conditions, treatment management is often a source of conflict. Parents can become frustrated with feeling that they need to frequently ask their adolescents to do the tasks that they already know how to do, and tweens can perceive these reminders as nagging. This can result in unhelpful parental approaches to illness management—being overly involved/intrusive or being overly permissive or "hands-off." It's also common for parents to swing from one to the other when they feel overwhelmed or frustrated with one approach or when they feel judged by others for how they are handling their child's health condition. Here are some helpful reminders:

1. **Find a balance.** A parent may be checking in with their tween multiple times a day by text or via phone, messaging with a school nurse, and communicating with coaches about the child's health condition, which could make the tween angry

and/or withdrawn. Or this parent may be tempted to let their adolescent deal with it on their own, withdrawing support. Neither of these extremes is helpful, however, as a collaborative approach has been shown to yield both better health outcomes and better of quality of life.

2. **Watch your tone.** If a parent thinks a child is skipping insulin due to laziness, their response is likely to be one of frustration or anger, whereas if they think it's happening because their child is overwhelmed or depressed, they are more likely to respond with compassion and support.

3. **Set up planned check-ins. A regular time to check in about diabetes** management, or other topics like grades, can be helpful. These are meant to be brief (two to three minutes) and constructive (finding solutions rather than bringing up past mistakes). With planned times to talk about a topic, you may feel less pressured to ask about it *every time* you see your child, and your kid will know that they are accountable because the conversation is already scheduled. Think about the tone and the context of your check-in. A positive example would be:

   > *"Looks like your blood sugar is high—any ideas about what's different today?"*

   A more accusatory or judgmental example would be:

   > *"Your blood sugar has been high all afternoon—what did you eat?!"*

4. **Tag-team your efforts with a partner.** In many families, one parent is most involved in the daily management of a chronic illness—asking about symptoms and whether the child has taken their medication, keeping track of medical appointments and supplies—and the other parent or caregiver may

only step in when things aren't going well. Trading off which parent/caregiver does the check-ins can be a great way to make sure all caregivers are involved and up to date on how management is going, while providing respite for the parent who is typically responsible for daily management.

Positive Reinforcement

Acknowledge that your child has more to deal with than their peers. They may have to get up earlier to take medications before eating, frequently leave class to go to the nurse, or have to take a break from doing something fun (playing a video game, swimming in a friend's pool) to take care of their health. It's a lot. And kids frequently feel that no one understands what it's like for them, so it is okay to offer special treats or rewards for the extra work that they do. These don't have to be expensive or time-consuming—it could be something like letting them choose what's for dinner or which movie you watch or taking them to the mall or community event. Some families of kids with diabetes have a party to celebrate the "diaversary" or date their child was diagnosed to acknowledge and celebrate all the work they do.

Decide on House Rules in Advance

To avoid frequent power struggles and arguments, decide on your "house rules," and make sure that your child knows what the rules are and why the rules exist. These can be rules about household chores (e.g., your child is responsible for feeding the dog every night and taking the trash out on Mondays), guests (e.g., your child must check with you before having friends over and an adult needs to be home if your child has guests), or related to their health care (e.g., you need to have a conversation with their friend's parent about diabetes management before your child can spend the night). Be sure to praise the behaviors you want to see in a specific, genuine way (e.g., "Thank you for taking out the trash"). And choose consequences for breaking the rules that you can enforce. For example, restricting them from video games for a weekend is much more feasible than grounding them for a month.

It is normal for tweens to test limits, take risks, and question the rules. This is also a time when your child may have constructive and creative solutions to getting things done, so be open to their ideas and input about the rules. Kids will notice if you follow through and are consistent in enforcing rules, and over time, they will push back less often if they know that the rules are firm and logical.

Encourage Independence

During adolescence, responsibility for treatment management typically shifts from the parent to the child. For some parents, it's challenging to let go of control, while others may relinquish responsibility too quickly. The successful transfer of responsibility is not a smooth, upward trajectory. There are likely to be some steps forward and some steps back. A parent may give a child more opportunities to manage on their own (e.g., going to a sleepover or on a school trip) and make adjustments if needed, but it is normal for kids to do well for a while and then hit a rough patch when they experience burnout or lack of motivation. It can be helpful to offer additional support at times you know your child may be experiencing extra stress (e.g., during a week of exams, tryouts for a team or school performance) or during times of transition (e.g., the start of a new school or new grade or the shift to a less structured summer schedule).

Keep in mind that simply knowing how to do the tasks of illness management does not mean that your child is ready to do it on their own. Most 12-year-olds could physically drive a car, but we don't let them get a driver's license until they have developed the maturity needed to handle the responsibility of driving. Kids with chronic health conditions need support for illness management throughout adolescence and even into adulthood.

Here are some good ways to shift responsibility from parent to teen incrementally:

- Meal planning: Bring your child to the grocery store to pick out foods for breakfast or lunch that they can prepare.
- Nonverbal communication: Set a phone reminder for taking insulin.
- Goal-setting (be as specific as possible): Have your child pack their own supplies and snacks for sports practice three days per week.
- Positive feedback: Reinforce your child's responsible behaviors.
- Guidance or advice when problems occur (without getting angry): Make an observation ("your blood sugar has been low the past few mornings") and listen without jumping in to solve the problem; see what ideas your child has for how to fix it.

Closing Advice

The suggestions offered in this chapter are based on both research and clinical experience, and they have been effective for many families. There will be times that you and your child are doing everything "right" and they will still experience an illness flare-up or other problem. There will also be times when you wish you had done something differently. The good news for chronic health conditions is that the daily tasks of management give you and your child so many opportunities to try new strategies or find new ways to work together to reach a balance between "perfect" management and a positive relationship and good quality of life.

www.ingramcontent.com/pod-product-compliance
Lightning Source LLC
Chambersburg PA
CBHW011758040426
42446CB00018B/3452